The Layman's Dictionary of
English Law

Gavin McFarlane

LL.M (Sheffield), Ph.D (London)
Barrister and Harmsworth Scholar of the Middle Temple

The Layman's Dictionary of
English Law

WATERLOW PUBLISHERS LIMITED

First Edition 1984
©Gavin McFarlane 1984
Waterlow Publishers Limited
Maxwell House
74 Worship Street
London EC2A 2EN
A member of the British Printing &
Communication Corporation PLC

British Library Cataloguing in Publication Data
   McFarlane, Gavin
      The layman's dictionary of English law.
   1.   Law—England—Dictionaries
   I.   Title
   344.208'6   KD313
      ISBN 0 08 039161 3 (Hardback)
         0 08 039157 5 (Paperback)

Cover photo:
Royal Courts of Justice, London
(Colour Library International)

Designed by the Graphic Partnership
Printed and bound in
Great Britain by
A. Wheaton & Co. Ltd., Exeter.

Preface

There is little doubt that across the centuries lawyers have tended to envelop their activities in a shroud of jargon which often mystifies the general public. Less true perhaps is the accusation that, having invented a private language, the legal profession then has to be paid substantial sums to explain what it is really talking about!

Most legal dictionaries until now have sought to provide a summary of the law relating to each entry, or to give the strict legal definition of each word or phrase. This is very helpful to other lawyers, but may not be of much assistance to the non-lawyer looking for a quick insight into the fundamentals. This Dictionary does not set out to provide definitions for citation in courts of law; on the contrary, it tries to convey a clear impression in everyday language of the terms and expressions commonly used in legal offices and documents. I hope that I have suceeded in avoiding any direct reference to a decided case or a particular Act of Parliament.

It has not been possible to escape completely from Latin tags and maxims, as they are so widely used by the legal profession. Side by side with the new concepts of consumer credit and software protection there are entries describing courts and legal principles which no longer apply in modern law. They are included because they are often referred to in the general literature of our language, and form part of the country's social and economic development.

This book is designed to find a place in the ordinary household, so that it may help to give a speedy explanation of legal words and phrases used in newspapers and broadcasting, or the technical documentation which increasingly finds it way through the letter box. I hope that it may also be of use to students of law and other professional disciplines, to the businessman or woman, and indeed to anyone brought into contact with our legal system.

It remains to acknowledge the friendly encouragement and assistance I have received from the editorial staff at Waterlows, particularly James Lamb, Jeremy Stratton and Kate Robertson.

G.McF.

In fond memory of my brother
Neil Stewart Robertson McFarlane
(1939-1952)

Abbreviations used in the Dictionary

(Fr.)   French (including Norman French)

(Lat.) Latin

(q.v.) quod vide, *which see* (a cross-reference which may prove
     helpful)

A

abandonment of claim

The relinquishment by one side in a civil action of its claim against the other side or party.

abatement

(1) The bringing to an end of a situation which was causing a nuisance.

(2) The proportionate reduction of all bequests in a will, where they cannot be paid in full.

abduction

The crime of taking a woman or girl away, or keeping her against her will for marriage or sexual purposes. In the case of a girl under 16, taking her away from the person responsible for her.

ab extra *(Lat.)*

From the outside.

ab inconvenienti *(Lat.)*

An argument which sets out to provide an explanation for a tricky problem.

ab initio *(Lat.)*

From the beginning; from the outset.

abominable crime

A nineteenth century expression used to describe BUGGERY (q.v.) and BESTIALITY (q.v.)

abortion
>The termination of pregnancy, which may constitute a crime if the prescribed conditions are not carried out.

absconding
>The act of making off without permission, applied frequently to people who have been released on bail.

absolute bill of sale
>A BILL OF SALE (q.v.) not given as security for money, which vests the property absolutely in the GRANTEE (q.v.), although the GRANTOR (q.v.) keeps possession.

absolute discharge
>An order made by a court in a criminal case whereby no immediate punishment is imposed on the person discharged.

absolute offence
>A criminal offence of so-called strict liability, in which no element of intention is needed in order to prove guilt.

absolute privilege
>A defence to an action for defamation where the words complained of were uttered during the course of one of a limited class of occasions, such as Parliamentary or judicial proceedings.

abstract of title
>In conveyancing, a document drawn up on behalf of the seller summarising the title deeds.

abuse of process
>Something done by the prosecution in a criminal trial which seriously prejudices the possibility of the accused person successfully defending himself.

abusing children
>The criminal offence of having unlawful intercourse with young girls.

abuttals
>The boundaries of any piece of land, at points where it touches neighbouring pieces of land.

academic lawyer

A teacher of law, not necessarily practising or employed in the law, but whose researches or commentaries may assist in its development.

A.C.A.S.

The Advisory, Conciliation and Arbitration Service, set up to work for improvement in industrial relations, particularly collective bargaining procedures.

accepting house

A business which guarantees payment of debts by accepting bills of exchange drawn on them by the sellers of goods.

acceptor

The term applied after his acceptance to the person (for example a bank) called on to make a payment under a cheque or a bill of exchange.

access

(1) A right enjoyed by all owners of land which adjoins a highway.

(2) In matrimonial proceedings, a right granted to a parent, who has not been awarded CARE AND CONTROL (q.v.), to come into contact with his or her child on a regular basis.

accident

A defence which may be successful in criminal cases where MENS REA (q.v.) is required, but which will not necessarily be effective in STRICT LIABILITY or ABSOLUTE OFFENCES (q.v.)

accident book

A record of all accidents which every person, company or business employing 10 or more people is obliged to keep.

accommodation bill

A negotiable instrument (bill of exchange) put into circulation without any CONSIDERATION (q.v.) having been given, in order to assist or accommodate the person principally involved.

accord and satisfaction

An agreement between persons who originally made a

contract, that it shall be carried out in a different way, and that no legal action will result because of it.

Accountant-General

The official who holds funds paid into court in any case or action taking place in the SUPREME COURT OF JUDICATURE (q.v.)

account payee only

A cheque with this crossing on it may only be paid into the account of the person specified. The bank receiving it is negligent if it pays it in to any other account.

accretion

The addition of new territory to the existing territory of a state by operation of nature, such as the emergence of a volcanic island in its territorial waters.

accused

The person against whom a criminal charge or prosecution is brought. Also called 'the defendant'. The term 'the prisoner' is now discouraged.

acquittal

A verdict in a criminal case meaning that the facts alleged against the person accused are not proved, and that accordingly he should not be convicted.

action in personam

A case against a person, as opposed to a case for the recovery of a certain thing or of goods.

action in rem

A case for the recovery of a certain thing or of goods, as opposed to a case against a person.

actionable per se

Applied to an action which can be brought but which requires the plaintiff to prove damage.

actio personalis moritur cum persona *(Lat.)*

A right of action to which an individual is entitled while alive, but which comes to an end on that person's death.

active partner

A member of a PARTNERSHIP (q.v.) who assumes executive responsibility for the business.

act of bankruptcy

One of a number of acts which may be committed by a debtor and giving rise to a bankruptcy petition. An example would be a fraudulent transfer of part of his property.

act of God

An act of fate or the workings of nature which causes some loss, damage or injury.

act of indemnity

A law passed by Parliament to pardon or legalise an illegal action taken in the past.

Act of Parliament

A written law which has passed through first, second and third readings in both Houses of Parliament, and has received the Royal Assent.

act of state

An exercise of power by the Sovereign which cannot be questioned in a court of law; a defence to an action in an English court in respect of an act committed abroad by a Crown servant.

actual bodily harm (ABH)

The crime of causing physical harm to another person, of a less serious kind than GRIEVOUS BODILY HARM (q.v.)

actual loss

The situation where no part of the subject-matter of a policy of insurance remains in existence.

actuary

A member of the actuarial profession. Not a lawyer, but concerned with calculations such as life expectancy and various probabilities for insurance purposes.

actus non facit reum, nisi mens sit rea *(Lat.)*

'An action does not make for guilt, unless there is a guilty intent.'

actus reus *(Lat.)*

An act which is forbidden for the purposes of the criminal law.

adaptation

The conversion of a copyright work, such as a novel, into another form, such as a play.

address for service

An address nominated by a party to a case, at which any document for him may be left.

ademption

The cancellation of a specific bequest in a will, because the object or funds referred to have already been disposed of during the life of the maker of the will.

ad hoc *(Lat.)*

For a specific case, in the sense of an arrangement or action taken to deal with a particular situation.

ad idem *(Lat.)*

In complete agreement.

ad infinitum *(Lat.)*

For ever.

adjacent zone

In international law, water outside the territorial limits of a particular state, where special interests may be claimed.

adjourned sine die

Adjournment without a day being fixed for the next hearing of a case; therefore adjourned indefinitely.

adjournment of the House

The ending of a sitting of the House of Lords or the House of Commons, generally on the basis that the next sitting will take place on the following working day.

adjudication order

A court order having the effect of judging a debtor bankrupt.

ad litem *(Lat.)*

For the purposes of the case being heard, for example a GUARDIAN AD LITEM (q.v.)

administrator

A person interested in an estate to whom letters of administration have been granted after the maker's death where probate could not be granted, usually because of intestacy.

administration ad litem

A special grant of administration for the purpose of litigation, where the proper executor or administrator will not assume responsibility.

administration cum testamento annexo

A grant of administration 'with the will attached', which has the same effect as a grant of probate. It is applicable where the person who has died has left a will, but there is no executor to take the grant.

administration de bonis non administratis

A special grant of administration over part of an estate not yet administered, on the death of an administrator or sole executor, provided that an original grant has already been made.

administration durante absentia

A special grant of administration while an executor or administrator is abroad.

administration durante dementia

A special grant of administration while the person otherwise entitled to it is suffering from a temporary mental disorder.

administration durante minore aetate

A special grant of administration during the minority of an executor or administrator.

administration order

A court order for the administration of the estate of someone who cannot meet the conditions of a court order made against him.

administration pendente lite
> A special grant of administration while litigation is pending over the validity of a will, or the revocation of a grant of probate.

administrative law
> The rules covering areas of legal control exercised by agencies other than courts which have the right to administer law. Much of this is concerned with tribunals.

administrative tribunals
> Bodies outside the ordinary judicial system of courts, set up under Acts of Parliament with judicial or similar powers.

administrator's oath
> A document filed in order to obtain a grant of administration, giving certain information about the relevant death.

Admiralty law
> The body of law arising out of shipping and maritime matters, including salvage and collisions at sea.

Admiralty Court
> Until 1873, the court which dealt with Admiralty matters. They were then transferred to the Probate, Divorce and Admiralty Division of the High Court.

Admiralty Court of the Cinque Ports
> A special court sitting to hear maritime matters arising within the jurisdiction of the Cinque Ports.

admission
> The acknowledgement by one side to a case and given to the other side, of the truth of certain matters which have been alleged.

adoption proceedings
> The system in the county courts by which the formal adoption of a child is carried out.

adoptive child
> Someone who has been legally adopted as another person's child.

adoptive parent
> Someone who has legally adopted another person as their child.

adultery
> Sexual relations by a married person with someone other than his or her spouse, now evidence of irretrievable breakdown of marriage.

ad valorem duty
> A duty payable on goods calculated as a percentage of their value.

ad valorem freight
> A charge for shipping goods by reference to a stated percentage of their value.

advance freight
> A sum to be paid in advance, in respect of the carriage of goods by sea.

advocate
> One who presents a case orally, as a barrister or solicitor; in Scotland, a member of the Faculty of Advocates, equivalent to a barrister in England and Wales.

advowson
> The right to nominate a clergyman to a particular church appointment.

affidavit
> A document sworn on oath before a Commissioner to administer oaths.

affidavit of alias
> An affidavit to be attached to an application for the grant of PROBATE (q.v.), where the maker of the will made use of an alias name.

affidavit of execution
> A document on oath certifying that a will was probably signed when some doubt existed about it.

affidavit of plight and condition
In cases involving wills which have been marked in some way, a document sworn on oath explaining how it got into that condition.

affiliate
A commercial organisation which is subject to the control or influence of another commercial organisation.

affiliation order
A court order made for the support of an illegitimate child by the person found to be its father.

affiliation proceedings
An action brought by the mother of a child against the man whom she alleges is its father, in order to establish paternity and obtain financial support.

affirmation
The alternative to the swearing of an OATH (q.v.) in judicial proceedings, either where the person making the declaration does not wish to swear on the basis of religious belief, or where it is not practicable to administer the appropriate oath.

affreightment
The carriage of goods by sea in return for reward.

affray
A fight between two or more people which frightens members of the public, and constitutes a criminal offence.

a fortiori *(Lat.)*
With all the more reason (to emphasise a particular point).

agency
The relationship between one person (the AGENT, q.v.) authorised by another person (the PRINCIPAL, q.v.) to act on his behalf in matters relating to contracts.

agency by implication
An agency inferred in certain cases from the conduct of the persons concerned.

agency by ratification
> The situation where a person subsequently approves acts done on his behalf by another person which were not properly authorised.

agency of necessity
> Where in an emergency the powers of an agent are by implication of law conferred on a particular person.

agent
> An intermediary engaged by one person to bring about contractual relations on his behalf with someone else.

agent's advice note
> A document giving full particulars of cargo sent by an exporter to his forwarding agent.

age of consent
> The age (16) at which a girl can give her consent to sexual intercourse, without the man being liable to prosecution.

aggravated burglary
> Burglary carried out with the use of firearms or weapons.

agricultural tenancy
> A letting of premises or land to someone engaged in agricultural work.

aiding and abetting
> Assisting in a crime, now usually as a principal in the second degree.

agreed value clause
> A provision in a bill of lading limiting the carrier's liability to a fixed sum.

airside
> The area of an airport subject to customs control when an outgoing passenger has passed through customs.

air waybill
> A contractual document between shipper and carrier regulating the carriage of goods by air.

ale

Orginally applied to beer brewed without hops, but now included in the legal definition of beer.

alias

A fictitious or assumed name; 'otherwise known as'.

alibi

The contention by a person accused of a criminal offence that he was elsewhere at the relevant time.

alibi warning

Notice which the defence is obliged to give to the prosecution of its intention to plead an ALIBI (q.v.)

alien enemy

A foreigner with whose country war has broken out. He enjoys no rights or privileges in the United Kingdom in consequence.

alien friend

A foreigner who enjoys most rights of a citizen of the United Kingdom, except that he cannot vote or hold official office.

alimony pending suit

In matrimonial proceedings, the amount of financial provision which must be made by the husband while the case is being prepared for hearing.

aliter *(Lat.)*

On the contrary.

All England Law Reports

A modern series of comprehensive law reports, cited as 'All E.R.'

aliunde *(Lat.)*

From other sources.

allocatur *(Lat.)*

A certification given at the end of a court case by a TAXING MASTER (q.v.), showing the costs he has allowed.

allonge *(Fr.)*

A slip of paper attached to a BILL OF EXCHANGE (q.v.), on which a series of endorsers add their signatures.

allotted day

One of the days of Parliamentary time which must during each session be devoted to the supply of money to the Crown for funding the public service.

alongside date

The date when a ship is ready to take on cargo for exportation.

ambassador

A person exempt from civil and criminal proceedings as head of his country's diplomatic representation, together with other specified categories of diplomatic and similar personnel.

ambulatory will

A will which can still be altered or revoked because the maker has not yet died.

amendment

An alteration to a legal document or draft, or to a Bill on its way through Parliament.

a mensa et thoro *(Lat.)*

'From table and bed'. Used in matrimonial cases to describe a separation from one's spouse.

amicus curiae *(Lat.)*

'Friend of the court'. A barrister not directly concerned with a particular case, but who is invited to address the court because of special knowledge of some point arising in a case.

ancient lights

A notice of a claim by a landowner to a long-established and undisturbed right to light.

ancillary grant

An English grant of probate, where a foreigner has died leaving chattels in England, and a will has already been granted probate in the foreigner's country of domicile.

ancillary relief
> Matters relating to a family court's jurisdiction over maintenance and children.

animus deserendi *(Lat.)*
> The intention to desert.

animus manendi *(Lat.)*
> The intention to remain in a particular country, by which a person acquires a DOMICILE OF CHOICE (q.v.)

animus possedendi *(Lat.)*
> The intention to possess.

animus revertendi *(Lat.)*
> The intention to return.

animus revocandi *(Lat.)*
> The intention to revoke a will.

animus testandi *(Lat.)*
> The free and full intention to make a will, without which that will would be invalid.

annual general meeting
> A meeting which every company must hold each year, and which must take place within 15 months of the previous annual general meeting.

annual return
> A document which a company must file each year setting out particulars of addresses, directors, members and capital and of any debts owed to it.

annuitant
> The person due to receive payments under an ANNUITY (q.v.)

annuity
> A sum of money payable at intervals during the lifetime of the person due to receive it.

annulment of adjudication
> The cancellation of an order adjudging a debtor to be bankrupt.

annulment of marriage

A form of legal termination of a marriage so that for all practical purposes it never existed. To this extent it differs from a DIVORCE (q.v.)

answer

A form of reply by one party to matters formally alleged against him in legal pleadings.

ante *(Lat.)*

Before (usually in the sense of 'see previous reference').

antecedents

Details given to a court about to sentence a person guilty of a criminal offence, which relate to his record and background.

ante-dated cheque

A cheque bearing a date earlier than the date on which it was made out.

anticipation

The earlier use or publication of an invention in respect of which a patent is claimed, and which will cause the rejection of the claim.

anti-dumping duty

A charge levied by an importing country to counteract goods entering which appear to have been unfairly subsidised in the country of production.

ante-nuptial settlement

An agreement made before a marriage by one or both potential spouses to bring certain property into their joint control.

anti-trust legislation

A department of United States law designed to ensure fair competition. It can affect contracts between American and non-American companies where its principles are infringed.

Anton Piller order

A court order allowing the applicant to search premises for

certain kinds of evidence, and to seize it. Used to combat material which infringes copyright.

a posteriori *(Lat.)*
　　From subsequent conclusions.

a priori *(Lat.)*
　　From previous contentions.

appeal of felony
　　In medieval times, a private action which could be brought in the king's court claiming that someone had committed a felony.

appellant
　　A person who takes a case on appeal to a higher court.

appellate jurisdiction
　　The jurisdiction of a court to hear appeals from decisions of a lower court.

appraisement
　　The valuation of a ship or its cargo for the purposes of salvage.

appraiser
　　Someone who carries out the calling or occupation of APPRAISEMENT (q.v.) or valuation.

appropriation
　　The earmarking of money under Parliamentary authorisation for funding public expenditure.

appropriation accounts
　　Accounts made by the various Departments of State of the manner in which grants voted to them by Parliament have been spent.

appropriation in aid
　　The setting-off by a Department of State or Ministry of money it has received from outside sources, against money it would normally be due to receive from the Exchequer.

approved school
　　A corrective establishment for young offenders of school age.

aqua vitae *(Lat.)*

Originally applied for duty purposes to plain spirits distilled in the Scottish Lowlands, as opposed to 'uisge beatha' distilled in the Highlands.

arbitrage

The technique of dealing by taking profits in different places at the same time, due to anomalies in local prices or rates of exchange.

arbitration

A system of settling disputes outside the formal scheme of the courts. It is frequently used in commercial matters.

arbitrator

A kind of umpire or referee who with the agreement of both parties can settle a dispute outside the system of the civil courts.

Archdiaconal Court

Previously a minor ecclesiastical court presided over by the person nominated by an archdeacon.

Arches Court of Canterbury

An ecclesiastical court having jurisdiction in matters relating to clergy for the province of Canterbury.

arrack

For duty purposes, a spirit distilled from toddy, rice or palm pulp.

arraignment

Procedure in the Crown Court by which the statement of the offence in an indictment is read to the person accused, and he is asked how he pleads.

arrest

The physical apprehension of a person so that he may answer a criminal charge.

arrestable offence

A crime in respect of which an authorised person may make an arrest without a warrant.

arrest with a warrant

Arrest by a police officer or other authorised person under a warrant issued by a justice of the peace after hearing evidence on oath that a crime has been committed.

arrest without warrant

Apprehension by a police officer or other authorised person for a criminal offence defined as an arrestable offence, and therefore one for which arrest without warrant can be made.

arson

A criminal offence involving deliberately setting fire to an object.

articled clerk

A person serving a period of training with a qualified solicitor, prior to being admitted as a member of the solicitor's profession.

articles

A period of apprenticeship to be served by someone who wants to become a solicitor before he can be admitted to the profession.

articles of association

A company document defining the rights of its members as between themselves, and against the company, and the delegation of powers to the directors.

articles of partnership

A document embodying the conditions governing a particular partnership relationship.

artificial person

A legal person other than a human being, for example, a corporation.

artistic works

Paintings, sculptures, drawings, engravings, photographs and such matters, capable of being protected by **COPYRIGHT** (q.v.).

a similibus ad similia *(Lat.)*

From like to like.

asportatio *(Lat.)*

 The act of carrying off.

assault

 The attempt to apply unlawful force to the body of another person, and causing that person to fear violence.

assay office

 An office set up for the hall-marking of gold and silver plate in London and certain provincial cities.

assessed taxes

 Formerly applied to duties assessed according to the number of taxable articles kept by a particular person. An example was the window tax, assessed on the number of windows in a house.

assessor

 A person with special skills who may be appointed to assist a judge in certain types of case.

assignment

 A transfer of rights which has legal effect.

assisted person

 A person involved as a party in a case, who is in receipt of LEGAL AID (q.v.).

Assize Court

 Former criminal court for serious cases triable by jury. Assizes were arranged geographically in circuits. They have now been replaced by the Crown Courts.

assize rolls

 In medieval times, the records kept of cases heard by the judges travelling about the country.

Associate of the Crown Office

 An official sitting below the judge in the High Court, who administers the oath to witnesses, registers material produced to the court during the trial, and records the judgment.

assumpsit *(Lat.)*
> An ancient action in civil law for breach of a contract. Literally, 'he undertook'.

assurance (or insurance)
> The undertaking by one person (the assurer) to pay money or confer a benefit on another person (the assured) on the happening of a certain event to take place in the future (usually the death of a specified person).

assured
> A person standing to benefit under a contract of ASSURANCE (q.v.)

assurer
> A person undertaking to pay a certain sum or confer a benefit on another person (the assured) on the taking place of an event certain to happen in the future, generally the death of an nominated person.

attachment of earnings
> The power to enforce a financial penalty or court order by direct deductions from a person's wages or salary.

attaint
> An action which at one time could be brought against a jury which brought in a false verdict.

attempt
> A step taken towards the commission of a substantive criminal offence, which in certain circumstances may itself amount to a crime.

attendance allowance
> A state benefit payable to people who are severely disabled, either mentally or physically, and who have needed care for at least six months.

attendance centre
> A person under 21 may be sentenced to attend such a centre so that he loses his leisure, and may be guided to useful recreational activities.

attest

To sign as a witness to the signature of another person.

attestation

The act of witnessing a signature on a document. In the case of a will the document would be invalid without it.

Attorney-General

One of the two Law Officers of the Crown, and a political appointment. He is the head of the Bar of England and Wales, who advises certain Government Departments, and undertakes certain prosecutions for the Crown.

Attorney-General's reference

The procedure by which a point of law arising in a criminal case where the accused has been acquitted may be taken to the Court of Appeal by the Attorney-General for its opinion.

auction

A public sale of goods or estate by stroke of hammer or other recognised manner, at which the highest bidder is deemed to be the purchaser.

auctioneer

A person offering goods or property for sale by auction, with competitive bidding at which the purchaser is deemed to be the highest bidder.

audi alteram partem *(Lat.)*

The principle that both parties to a dispute should be given their say.

audience

The right to address a court in legal proceedings, generally confined to the party himself, or a barrister or solicitor acting on his behalf.

audit

The periodic examination of account books by an AUDITOR (q.v.), to verify that they are correctly made up.

auditors
> Qualified accountants independent of a company who must be retained to report on its accounts.

auditor's report
> A statement which must be put before the general meeting of a company each year giving the opinion of the AUDITORS (q.v.) as to whether the accounts have been properly kept.

audit querela *(Lat.)*
> A form of assistance in medieval times for a defendant, who because of matters coming to light after the end of a case appeared to have been treated harshly.

aulnager
> The holder of a medieval office for the management and taxation of imported cloth.

authorised capital
> The nominal value of shares which a limited company is permitted by its MEMORANDUM OF ASSOCIATION (q.v.) to issue. Known also as nominal capital.

authorised clerk
> An employee of a stockbroking firm authorised to buy and sell shares on behalf of his employer.

Authors' Lending and Copyright Society (A.L.C.S.)
> A body set up to administer for authors any rights in the nature of copyright which may develop as technology introduces new ways of using copyright works.

authors' society
> A body responsible for the collection and distribution of royalties arising from the use of works protected by copyright.

automatism
> A condition whereby a person has no mental control over his movements.

autonomic legislation
> The power of an autonomous body such as a club or a professional association to make rules governing its members.

autrefois acquit *(Fr.)*

A contention by a person accused of a criminal offence that he has already been found not guilty of the charge.

autrefois convict *(Fr.)*

A contention by a person accused of a criminal offence that he has already been tried for it and convicted.

average

In contracts of marine insurance, an expression meaning loss or damage.

average clause

A clause in an insurance policy providing that if the value of property exceeds the amount for which it is insured, the insurer is only liable in the proportion which the sum insured bears to the property.

a vinculo matrimonii *(Lat.)*

'From the chains of marriage'. An expression used in the old ecclesiastical courts to describe a complete divorce, as opposed to JUDICIAL SEPARATION (q.v.)

B

bachelor duty

A tax imposed in 1695 on every bachelor over the age of 25, at a rate on a sliding scale according to his social position. It was abolished in 1706.

back freight

An amount due to a shipowner in a contract for the carriage of goods by sea, where goods have been carried beyond their original destination because it was not possible to deliver them.

background music

Music on a film soundtrack not intended to be heard by the actors, which attracts copyright royalties at a lower rate than FEATURE MUSIC (q.v.)

backwardation

A payment made by a person who has agreed to sell shares which he does not own, in order to carry the matter over into the next settlement period.

bail

The grant of liberty to an accused person pending trial, generally subject to conditions.

bailee

The person to whom goods are delivered on condition that they will be returned to the person who delivered them when the purpose of the delivery has been fulfilled.

bailiff
> A court official responsible for serving court documents, and enforcing its judgements by taking away goods under execution.

bailment
> A delivery of goods by one person, the bailor, to another person, the bailee, on condition that they shall be returned as soon as the purpose of the bailment is fulfilled.

bailor
> A person who delivers goods to another person (the bailee), on condition that they will be returned when the purpose of the delivery (bailment) has been fulfilled.

balance order
> An order made by the court in chambers on the application of the liquidator to enforce a call on shares not fully paid up during a winding-up.

balance sheet
> A statement which the directors of a company must put before its members each year in general meeting, giving a true picture of its affairs.

Baltic Exchange
> A London market for dealing in grain to be delivered at some time in the future.

banker's books
> A bank's official record of its customer's accounts, production of which in evidence may in some circumstances be enforced by court order.

banker's confirmed credit
> An arrangement between the purchaser of goods and his banker that a sum of money will be paid to the seller of the goods, on presentment to the bank of certain documents of authority.

banker's draft
> A draft for a sum of money drawn on a particular office of a

bank which is payable immediately to the person due to receive it.

bankrupt

A debtor against whom an adjudication order has been made.

bankruptcy petition

The procedure by which a creditor asks the Bankruptcy Court to issue a receiving order against a debtor.

Bar

Collectively, the profession of barristers. It is also used loosely to refer to the place in court from which advocates make their speeches.

Bar Association for Commerce, Finance and Industry (B.A.C.F.I.)

An association representing salaried barristers employed in the private sector.

Baron of Exchequer

A judge of the old Exchequer Court, which dealt with revenue cases.

barratry

A deliberate act of fraud or wrongdoing by a ship's master and/or a crew, by which the owners or charterers of a ship are damaged.

barring the entail

To obtain a fee simple in remainder, which takes effect on the death of the father concerned.

barrister

A member of one of the two branches of the legal profession. He may only receive work from a solicitor or patent agent, and has the exclusive right to conduct cases in the higher courts.

barter

A contract to pay for the purchase of goods with other goods rather than money.

bastard sugar

For duty purposes, lump sugar broken into pieces.

bastard wine

For duty purposes, wine which has been mixed or sweetened.

bastardy

Formerly, the condition of being born out of marriage, or illegitimate.

battery

The carrying out of the threat involved in an assault by coming into physical contact with another person.

bear

A person selling shares on the Stock Exchange in the hope of buying them back at a lower price. The seller may not necessarily own the shares, but looks for a profit on a falling market before he has to pay for them.

bearer

The person in possession of a particular document. Some documents such as bearer bills and bearer debentures may be claimed by any person possessing them.

bearer cheque

A cheque which can be negotiated (cashed or paid to his account) by the bearer.

bearer security (bearer bond)

Stocks or shares the title to which is evidenced by a bond conferring ownership on the person holding it for the time being.

beetroot distillery

Premises on which the distillation of spirits from beetroots was commenced experimentally in 1856, and therefore potentially a source of duty revenue to the Crown. It was abandoned in 1863 as unremunerative.

belligerent

A state actively engaged in war with another state.

Bencher

A senior barrister forming part of the governing body of his Inn of Court, and having disciplinary powers over its members.

bench warrant

An order issued by a court for the arrest of an ACCUSED (q.v.) who has not appeared at the appointed time to answer a criminal charge.

benefit of clergy

A device available in medieval times to those who had been sentenced to death, from which fate they could escape by demonstrating an ability to read.

beneficial contract of service

A contract relating to a young person's employment, which can be enforced against him because it is considered to be in his interests.

beneficiary

One on whose behalf property is held or administered by another person bound in conscience; a CESTUI QUE TRUST (q.v.)

Benelux

The three countries of Belgium, Holland and Luxembourg considered or acting together.

bequest

The making of a gift by will.

Berne Union

The main international copyright convention.

bestiality

Sexual intercourse between humans and animals, which is a crime where the human participant is a male.

best evidence

A rule of the law of evidence that the best means of proof must be given which the nature of the case allows.

betting duty

A tax charged on bets made with a bookmaker, both on racecourses and in betting-shops.

bicameralism
> The principle of having two chambers or houses in a parliamentary system.

bigamy
> The act of going through another ceremony of marriage while one's first spouse is still alive and no divorce has been obtained.

bill broker
> A retailing dealer in Treausury bills, who buys them outright, and profits by selling on any alteration in discount rates.

billeting
> The power enjoyed by the state in times of emergency to make householders give board and lodging to members of the armed forces.

bill in eyre
> A simple petition for the righting of an injustice which could be made in the Middle Ages.

bill of exception
> A direction or ruling by a judge which did not appear on the official record of a case. Now abolished.

bill of exchange
> An unconditional written order addressed by one person to another, and signed by the person giving it, which requires the person to whom it is addressed to pay either on demand or at a particular time in the future a certain sum of money to either a particular person or his order, or to the person holding the bill of exchange.

bill of exchange policy
> A form of bad debt insurance covering losses on bills of exchange drawn by the insured person.

bill of health
> A certificate of freedom from disease issued on request at the port of clearance to the master of a ship sailing to a foreign destination in which quarantine regulations are observed.

bill of lading

> A document recording the loading of goods onto a ship, with particulars of the terms agreed as to their carriage.

bill of lading in blank

> A BILL OF LADING (q.v.) which may be freely transferred from hand to hand.

bill of sale

> Effected in connection with a loan, so as to transfer owner-ship of the object put up as security to the lender, while possession of the object stays with the borrower.

bill of sight

> A provisional customs entry allowing an importer to land and examine goods under surveillance when he has not sufficient information to make a declaration without examination.

bill of store

> A customs entry for the re-importation of goods which have been exported within the previous five years.

binding over

> A power vested in magistrates to require a person to keep the peace and be of good behaviour. It does not depend on a conviction, and may be imposed on someone found not guilty.

binding precedent

> A decision of a higher court which a lower court is bound to follow.

bingo duty

> A tax payable by the promoter of a game of bingo.

birth duty

> A tax imposed in 1695 on parents on a sliding scale according to their social standing in respect of the birth of every child. It was abolished in 1706.

blackmail

> An unjustified demand accompanied by threats in order to obtain advantage to oneself or to cause loss to another.

Black Rod

The official of Parliament who conducts the SPEAKER OF THE HOUSE OF COMMONS (q.v.) to the House of Lords.

blank cheque

A cheque which has been signed by the authorised person, but with the amount payable left blank to be filled in later.

blank transfer

A transfer document in connection with a loan made on the security of shares which is signed by the borrower but with the name of the transferee left blank. In the event of default by the borrower this is filled in to secure transfer of the shares to the lender.

blocked currency

The system adopted by certain states of paying money due to a foreign creditor into a special 'blocked account', which the creditor can only use for a restricted range of purposes.

blocking a bill

A procedure to impede the consideration of a bill at a sitting of the House of Commons, on the objection of a Member of Parliament.

blood test

An aid to establishing the paternity of a child in AFFILIATION PROCEEDINGS (q.v.)

blue bag

The bag in which a newly called (or if he has had it for many years, by inference an unsuccessful) junior barrister carries his robes. (q.v. RED BAG.)

boarding station

A place appointed at every port in the United Kingdom at which ships arriving from a destination abroad must bring to for the boarding or landing of customs officers.

bona fides *(Lat.)*

Good faith.

bona vacantia *(Lat.)*

Property without an owner, and which no one is entitled to inherit.

bond

Personal security for the payment of money or the carrying out of an act.

bonded goods

Goods which for the purposes of release from duty have been subject to the payment of a bond by way of security.

bonded warehouse

Premises approved for the containing of BONDED GOODS (q.v.)

bonus shares

An issue of fully paid-up shares to a company's shareholders, issued from profits which have been retained in the past.

book debts

Those sums shown in a trader's accounts as being money due to him.

book entry

An entry made in accounts merely for the purposes of adjustment.

books duty

A customs duty on imported books first imposed in 1660, and abolished in 1861.

books of account

Records of receipts, expenditure, sales, purchases, assets and liabilities which a company is obliged to maintain in a proper manner.

book value

The valuation of a property belonging to a business enterprise as it is given in its accounts.

bootlegging

In copyright law, the release without authorisation of recordings of musical performances, for example rehearsals or private recordings taken surreptitiously of live concerts. It is derived from the popular expression for the illicit distillation of alcohol.

Borough Court

An early form of court which in the Middle Ages heard both civil and criminal cases within the confines of a borough.

Borstal

Formerly, an establishment for the corrective training of young offenders. Borstal sentences have now been replaced by the YOUTH CUSTODY ORDER (q.v.)

bot

In the Middle Ages, compensation payable for an injury or wrongdoing.

bottomry bond

A form of security pledging a ship and/or its cargo for the repayment of money borrowed for the purposes of a voyage.

bought note

A note of the terms of a transaction on the Stock Exchange, rendered by a stockbroker to his client.

boundary

An imaginary line delimiting the area of land owned or under occupation.

Boundary Commission

A body which reviews the representation of the House of Commons, and the number and extent of its constituencies.

breach of trust

An improper act, neglect or default on the part of a trustee in connection with his duties in relation to a trust.

break clause

A provision in a contract permitting either side to bring it to an end.

breaking bulk

The act of starting the unloading of a ship.

bribe

A corrupt inducement to persuade the person receiving it to behave in a particular way.

bribery

The giving or receiving of a bribe, which constitutes a criminal offence under the prevention of corruption legislation.

brief

Formal written instructions delivered by a solicitor to a barrister whom he has retained or instructed to act for his lay client.

British Standards Institution

The body responsible for drawing up national standards for products in the United Kingdom.

broadcasting right

The right to forbid or allow the broadcasting of a work subject to copyright control.

brokerage

A commission paid to a stockbroker by a company issuing shares, where the broker's clients have applied for shares.

Brussels Tariff Nomenclature

The standard classification of goods for the purpose of customs tariffs which is most widely used internationally.

brutum fulmen *(Lat.)*

A toothless threat.

budget

A collection of proposals put forward by the Chancellor of the Exchequer to control the expenditure of the state, generally on an annual basis.

buggery

Sexual intercourse by a male person involving anal penetration.

bull

> A person who purchases shares on the Stock Exchange in the hope that the price will rise sufficiently to allow him to make a profit before he has to pay for them.

bullion

> Unrefined gold and silver in dust, amalgam or lumps and bars, and refined gold or silver in bars.

burden of proof

> The onus of establishing that a particular argument is correct.

burglary

> Entering any building as a trespasser with the intention either of stealing something in it, or of inflicting grievous bodily harm, or raping any woman there, or doing unlawful damage.

burial duty

> A tax imposed in 1695 on the burial of every person at a varying rate according to their social position. It was abolished in 1706.

business name

> The name or style under which any business is carried on, either as a company or partnership, or under a sole proprietor.

butlerage (also prisage)

> Wine taken by the King's Butler in the Middle Ages for the king's use, from every ship bringing wine into the country.

bye-laws

> A form of DELEGATED LEGISLATION (q.v.) made by local authorities, usually requiring confirmation by a Ministry or Department of State.

C

Cabinet
The nerve centre of the government, chosen by the Prime Minister from his or her senior colleagues.

Cabinet Secretariat
A body servicing and supporting the meetings of the Cabinet.

c.a.d. (cash against documents)
A procedure by which a bank will only hand over documents giving title to goods under a contract on receipt of money.

cadit quaestio *(Lat.)*
'There can be no further argument in the matter.'

caeterorum *(Lat.)*
'Of the matters remaining.'

called-up capital
That section of the shareholding which has been called up on the shares issued. They are not therefore fully paid-up, and are liable to further calls.

calling aircraft
An aircraft flying between two foreign destinations which lands in the U.K. only in an emergency or for supplies, without loading or unloading freight or passengers.

calling ship
A ship coming from abroad into a port only for bunkering or

taking on stores, and which does not remain there more than 24 hours.

call on shares

A demand made by a limited company by resolution in accordance with its articles for any unpaid balance of the nominal value of shares.

C.A.N. (Customs Assigned Number)

A system of allocating numbers for endorsement on export documentation so that statistical information can be collected.

c. & f. (cost and freight)

A contract by which the seller undertakes to deliver goods on board ship for a particular destination, and pay the freight and the cost of unloading the goods on their arrival at that destination.

canon law

A system of ecclesiastical law having its roots in Roman law, once of wide application, but now very limited.

capacity

The ability of a person to enter into legal relations (such as a contract) or to meet legal obligations.

capias ad satisfaciendum *(Lat.)*

A writ authorising the seizure of the defendant in person, so that he may compensate for the harm suffered by the claimant.

capital assets

The property owned by a limited company.

capital clause

The clause in a company's memorandum of association which sets out the amount of nominal capital with which a company is to be registered, and how that capital is to be divided.

capital gains tax

A tax on chargeable gains (or capital profits) arising on the disposal of assets.

capitalisation of profits

The conversion of a company's profits into capital instead of paying them as dividends. This may be achieved by the issue of bonus shares or the discharge of shareholders' liability on shares not fully paid up.

capital murder

Murder punishable by death.

capital punishment

The ultimate penalty of death, abolished in the United Kingdom except in the case of treason.

capital redemption fund

A fund which must be established by a company out of undistributed profits, where REDEEMABLE PREFERENCE SHARES (q.v.) are to be redeemed from sources other than a fresh issue.

capital reserve

That part of the reserves of a limited company arising from the sale of shares for more than their nominal value. It may not be distributed except on liquidation.

captain's protest

Sworn statement by a ship's captain for insurance purposes, giving full details relating to a loss.

care and control

In matrimonial proceedings, the right of physical possession of children, as opposed to the formal legal control or CUSTODY (q.v.)

care proceedings

Court procedure to secure the welfare of a child who is alleged to be in need of care and protection.

cargo lien

A charge which may be levied against cargo for special services which have not been paid for.

carnal knowledge

Sexual intercourse, whether or not completed.

casus omissus *(Lat.)*

A gap or lacuna, particularly in an Act of Parliament.

cartel

An agreement between business organisations independent of each other to share the market between them.

cash with order

A term of a contractual offer indicating that if a payment is not made with the order which accepts the offer, then the goods will not be sent.

causa proxima *(Lat.)*

The immediate cause.

caveat *(Lat.)*

A written notice or warning. In probate, directed particularly to the Registrar warning him not to grant probate without giving notice to the person lodging the warning (the caveator).

caveat emptor *(Lat.)*

The principle that a buyer should take care to watch out for any defects, implying that he should bear the consequences of any which he fails to notice.

caveator *(Lat.)*

A person issuing a warning to a registrar not to grant probate without giving notice to him.

Central Criminal Court

The senior criminal court for Greater London, familiarly known as the Old Bailey.

certainties of trust

The elements of intention, subject-matter and objects which are essential to the creation of a valid trust.

certificate of age

A customs certification of the period for which certain spirits for export have been stored in wood and in bond in the United Kingdom.

certificate of incorporation

The document issued by the Registrar of Companies evidencing that all formalities of registration of a company have been complied with.

certificate of judgement

Official document recording the judgement of the High Court, to be stamped and served on the side losing a case.

certificate of origin

A certificate in prescribed form stating the country in which imported goods were grown, produced or manufactured.

certificate of pratique

A pass issued by customs allowing a ship arriving from abroad to proceed to a berth in port.

certificate of registry

The document issued by a Registrar on the completion of the registration of a British ship.

certificate of survey

A certificate issued after the surveying of a ship containing all the particulars required to be entered on the registration documents of a British ship.

certification of transfer

A procedure of the Stock Exchange for ensuring that irregularities or incomplete information does not hold up the delivery of shares on their transfer.

certiorari *(Lat.)*

A order of the High Court to review proceedings where there is a suggestion of bias, excess of jurisdiction, or an error on the record.

cessante ratione legis, cessat lex ipsa *(Lat.)*

Where the justification for a law ends, the law itself lapses.

cessate grant

A grant of probate made on the conclusion of a special grant made for a special reason, such as the minority or insanity of an executor.

cesser clause
A clause in a contract for the carriage of goods by sea, providing for the end of the charterer's liability when the goods are loaded on to the ship.

cession
In international law, a method of transferring territory from one state to another.

cestui que trust
One on whose behalf property is held or administered by another person bound in conscience; a beneficiary.

chain of representation
The transmission of executorship from one sole executor on his death to another executor previously appointed by the first as his successor.

Chairman of Ways and Means
The ex-officio chairman of all committees of the House of Commons, who also acts as Deputy Speaker.

chaldron of coal
36 bushels of coal, heaped up.

challenge for cause
An objection by the defence to a particular juror, with the reason being stated.

challenge without cause
An objection by the defence to a particular juror without the reason being stated.

challenge to the array
An objection by the defence to all the jurors who have been empanelled.

challenge to the polls
An objection by the defence to a particular juror.

chambers
>(1) A set of offices from which practising barristers work.
>(2) The venue for private hearings by judges, which are not taken in open court.

champertous
>Connected with CHAMPERTY (q.v.).

champerty
>A former offence committed by two or more persons agreeing to divide any proceeds of a legal action between them.

Chancellor of the Exchequer
>The Minister who is political chief of the TREASURY (q.v.) and responsible for control of national expenditure.

chance medley
>A killing in self-defence committed by a person who previously declined to take part in a brawl.

Chancery Bar
>The group of barristers who specialise in matters taken in the Chancery Division of the High Court, such as trusts and wills.

Chancery Court of York
>An ecclesiastical court having jurisdiction in matters relating to the clergy for the province of York.

Chancery Division
>The section of the High Court dealing chiefly with equitable matters such as trusts and administration of estates; also patents and contentious probate.

Chancery Master
>An official who hears summonses in the Chancery Division. Appointed from solicitors, he inspects accounts and conducts enquiries at the direction of a judge of the Chancery Division.

Channel Islands
>The islands of Guernsey, Jersey, Alderney, Sark and their respective dependencies. They do not form part of the United Kingdom.

charge

(1) A liability in respect of the property of a person or company, for example by making it the security for a loan by way of mortgage.

(2) Formal accusation of having committed a criminal offence.

charges clause

A provision in a contractual document setting out who is to bear the cost of specified items.

Charges Register

One of the Land Registers detailing all incumbrances on registered land such as mortgages or deposits.

charging order

A procedure against a judgement debtor for seizing stocks and shares, or his partnership interest in a firm.

charitable trust

A public trust for the relief of poverty, the advancement of religion, the advancement of education, or any other purpose beneficial to the community.

Charity Commissioners

Officials having wide powers to set up schemes for the administration of charitable property and trusts.

charter commission

The amount to be paid by a shipowner to a broker who has obtained a charter for his ship.

Chartered Institute of Patent Agents

The professional association regulating the practice and affairs of PATENT AGENTS (q.v.)

charterer

A person making a contract with a shipowner for the carriage of goods by sea (charterparty).

charterparty

A contract by which a shipowner agrees to place his vessel at the disposal of another person (charterer) for the carriage of goods by sea.

chattels real
Leaseholds.

cheap money
Money borrowed at a low rate of interest.

cheque
Legally a BILL OF EXCHANGE (q.v.) which requires a banker to pay a sum of money on demand to the drawer or a third party or to the bearer.

cheque card
A device to increase the acceptability of cheques by backing them (up to a certain amount) with the credit of the issuing bank.

cheque payable to order
A cheque which can only be negotiated by signature and delivery.

Chief Baron
Formerly the chief judge of the old Court of Exchequer.

Chief Land Registrar
The official at the head of the national system of land registration.

Chief Registrar of Shipping
The holder for the time being of the office of Collector of Customs and Excise, London Port.

child benefit
A state benefit payable to the mother of or other person responsible for a child under the qualifying age.

child of the family
In domestic proceedings, a child accepted as one of the family.

Chiltern Hundreds
One of the nominal offices of profit under the Crown, by

accepting which a Member of Parliament disqualifies himself and can thus resign his seat.

chose in action
An item of personal property not in physical or tangible form. Examples are company shares and copyrights, where formal transfer by assignment is needed.

chose in possession
A tangible physical object which can be transferred informally by gift or sale.

Church Assembly
A body of the established Church of England enjoying the right to pass measures having the force of law. Now known as the General Synod.

c.i.f. (cost, insurance, freight)
A contract by which a seller agrees to deliver goods on board ship for a particular destination, meet freight charges and take out at his expense a policy of marine insurance against the risks of the voyage.

c.i.f. & e. (cost, insurance, freight and exchange)
A contract by which the seller bears costs of insurance and freight, and in addition the risk of exchange fluctuations.

c.i.f.i. (cost, insurance, freight and interest)
A type of contract in which, in addition to freight and insurance, interest is added to the value of the shipment.

circuit
One of the six regions into which the business of the higher courts and the Bar is divided in England and Wales.

circuit administrator
The chief administrator of one of the six CIRCUITS (q.v.) among which higher court work outside London is divided.

circuit judge
The rank of judicial officer presiding in Crown Courts and County Courts.

circular issue

An invitation sent to existing shareholders of a company informing them of their entitlement to apply for new shares.

circulating capital

That part of the property of a company which has been acquired or brought into existence in order to dispose of it, hopefully for profit.

circumstantial evidence

Facts put forward as a means of proving an allegation by implication rather than direct evidence.

citation

(1) A notice issued by a person seeking a grant of probate or letters of administration to all others having a prior claim.

(2) Quoting of a decided case as authority for an argument.

citizen's arrest

One of a limited number of situations where a member of the public can make an arrest without warrant.

City of London Police

A branch of the professional police operating in the City of London, whose Chief Constable is appointed by the Common Council of the City.

Civil Contingencies Fund

A reserve fund to allow Departments of State and Ministries to meet emergency expenditure which has not had time to receive Parliamentary authorisation.

civil jury

A jury empanelled to try a dispute in a civil action, as opposed to a criminal case. It is now rarely used.

Civil List

The annual income of the sovereign and certain members of the sovereign's family, voted to provide for their needs and expenses.

clausula rebus sic stantibus *(Lat.)*

A doctrine of international law that a treaty is only binding so long as things stay as they are.

clean bill of health

A certificate that a ship left a particular port at a time when there was no infectious disease there.

clean bill of lading

A BILL OF LADING (q.v.) containing no qualification about the condition of the goods or their packing.

clearance inwards

The clearance through customs of arrivals from abroad.

clearance outwards

Customs authority for departure from a place in the United Kingdom for a destination abroad.

clearing bank

One of the main national banks which form an association of clearing houses; they exchange and settle orders for payment (cheques) drawn on them.

Clerk Assistant

The deputy to the chief permanent official of the House of Commons. A similar office exists in the House of Lords.

Clerk of the House of Commons

The head of the permanent staff of the House of Commons.

Clerk of the Parliaments

The official of the House of Lords who is the chief officer of the permanent staff.

clog on the equity

An unreasonable restriction of a person's rights which will in certain circumstances be set aside by the courts.

close company

A company controlled by five or fewer people.

closed fund policy

A policy of life assurance issued by a company which has been taken over, and which does no new business.

closed shop

A situation where it is made a condition of an individual's employment that he must be a member of or will join a particular trade union.

closure

A device of Parliamentary procedure to bring a debate to an end.

Coastguard

A customs staff originally formed in 1822 by amalgamating the Preventive Waterguard, Revenue Cruisers and Riding Officers. Management was transferred to the Admiralty in 1856, and to the Board of Trade in 1925.

coasting trade

Trade by sea between two ports in the United Kingdom.

codicil

A valid alteration or addition to a will made after it has been signed.

codified

Applied to an Act of Parliament which has drawn together all previous case and statute law on a subject; also used in Britain to distinguish foreign legal systems based entirely on written laws.

codifying statute

An Act of Parliament which gathers together all existing law on a particular subject, both in other Acts and in cases, so as to present a complete body of law.

coercion

A defence sometimes raised in criminal cases, rarely successfully, to the effect that the person accused was forced to act as he did.

cognating

In patent applications, the filing of a main claim which takes account of related modifications.

coinage offences
Criminal offences related to the counterfeiting and defacing of coinage.

coitus interruptus *(Lat.)*
Sexual intercourse which is not completed by an ejaculation on the part of the male.

Collector of Customs and Excise
The controller of a regional division of the Department of Customs and Excise; the highest rank in the regions of the Department outside London.

Colonial Legal Service
A body of salaried lawyers formerly recruited to staff the legal systems of what were once the British colonial territories.

colore officii *(Lat.)*
Under authority of a person's official position.

collusion
In international law, the arranging between the parties of the grounds for divorce, which could in certain circumstances prejudice matters.

Comecon
An economic grouping of Communist East European countries, broadly equivalent to the Common Market in Western Europe.

commencement date
The date at which an Act of Parliament comes into force, and is applied.

commercial blockade
A technique employed by nations during hostilities, by which one state closes the ports of the other to foreign trade.

Commercial Court
For cases in the QUEENS BENCH DIVISION (q.v.) of a specialised commercial subject-matter.

commission agent

A representative or agent who acts for an agreed commission, frequently on behalf of a foreign principal.

commissioner for oaths

An official appointed by the Lord Chancellor to supervise the formal swearing of oaths; he is almost invariably a solicitor.

Commissioners of Customs and Excise

Collectively, the Board of Customs and Excise.

Commissioners of Inland Revenue

Collectively, the Board of Inland Revenue.

Commission for Racial Equality

An official body which operates to prevent discrimination on the grounds of colour, race, nationality or ethnic origin.

commission of assize

The ancient system of sending High Court judges round the country on circuit to hear cases at certain towns.

Commission of General Gaol Delivery

One of the ancient commissions of the courts of assize, exercising jurisdiction to try serious criminal cases. Now performed by the High Court.

Commission of Oyer and Terminer

One of the ancient commissions of the courts of assize which exercised jurisdiction to try serious criminal cases. The High Court now performs this function.

Commission of the E.E.C.

The executive body of the Common Market, which initiates its policy, and drafts proposals to carry it out.

committal order

An order committing a person to prison for contempt of court.

committal proceedings

A hearing before magistrates to establish whether there is sufficient evidence of a serious crime to justify a trial by jury.

Committee for the Journals

A committee of the House of Lords which in theory is responsible for overseeing the JOURNALS (q.v.)

Committee Office

A department under the authority of the Clerk of the House of Commons.

committee of inspection

A group of CREDITORS and CONTRIBUTORIES (q.v.) appointed by the Court in a winding-up to oversee matters and control the liquidator.

Committee of Privileges

A SELECT COMMITTEE (q.v.) of the House of Commons dealing with allegations of breach of privilege.

Committe of Public Accounts

A committee of M.P.s of all parties which examines the appropriation accounts made by the various Departments of State.

Committee of Selection

A parliamentary committee whose duties are to appoint the members of standing and select committees.

committee stage

The clause by clause examination of proposed legislation in Bills before Parliament, sometimes carried out, not by the whole House, but by a committee.

Common Agricultural Policy

A cornerstone of the Common Market, aiming to stabilise food prices and guarantee the income of food producers.

common assault

The offence of using or threatening force against another person.

common barrator

A provoker of quarrels or law suits. No longer an offence since 1967.

common carrier

A person undertaking to transport the person or goods of anyone who chooses to employ him and who is able to pay his charges.

common duty of care

The duty of an occupier of premises to take reasonable care for the safety of a visitor there.

common employment

Employment so closely connected that the risk of an accident to one worker being caused by a fellow worker should have been forseen by the injured worker. The rule was abolished in 1948.

common fund costs

Costs allowed on the basis of all expenses which a solicitor would reasonably incur in the conduct of a case.

common law

Strictly, the general law contained in decided cases, as opposed to Acts of Parliament. But also used to include law in Acts of Parliament and decided cases as a contrast with EQUITY (q.v.) A third use is to distinguish the English (common-law) legal system from a foreign (codified) system of law.

common law cheat

An ancient criminal offence covering a wide range of deceptions which has now been replaced by modern statutory offences.

common law corporation

Created by express or presumed charter of the Monarch, such as the Corporation of the City of London.

Common Market Law Reports (CMLR)

A series of published decisions in cases relating to matters of EEC interest.

common night walker

Someone liable to disturb the peace, who sleeps in the day, and goes about at night-time. No longer an offence since 1967.

common scold

A trouble-making woman creating discord among her neigh-bours, and until 1967 creating a criminal offence by this behaviour.

common seal

The mark of corporate personality, which every registered limited company must possess. The company name must be legibly engraved on it.

Common Serjeant

A senior barrister exercising special judicial funcions in the Central Criminal Court (Old Bailey), and also the Mayor's and City of London Court.

Commonwealth

A loose and informal association of nations and territories having some link with the United Kingdom, and acknowledging its sovereign as head of the Commonwealth.

commorientes *(Lat.)*

Two people closely related who have died in the same disaster and in respect of whom it is necessary to decide who died first.

Community resources

The income funding the Common Market, derived from import duties and levies and national value added tax.

community service order

A punishment imposed by a criminal court whereby the person sentenced must attend a particular place to carry out a prescribed amount of unpaid work.

commutation

Part of the Royal Prerogative, by which a lesser punishment is substituted for a greater one.

Companies Liquidation Account

An account maintained at the Bank of England into which a liquidator is obliged to pay all the money he receives during the course of a winding up of a company.

company director
> A senior commercial manager of a trading concern subject to obligations and rights under company legislation.

company member
> A shareholder in a company limited by shares.

company promotion
> The procedure by which a company is incorporated by registration and established as a going concern.

company secretary
> An officer who must be engaged by every limited company. His office cannot be filled by a sole director. He is responsible for certain duties laid down by the Companies Acts.

compellability
> The condition of obligation to give evidence imposed on a person summoned as a witness in a case.

compensating products
> Goods which have been exported from the United Kingdom in another form and which, after processing abroad, have been returned to the United Kingdom.

compensation for loss of office
> Compensation paid to a director of a company who loses his position.

compensation fund
> A fund operated by the LAW SOCIETY (q.v.), to which all practising solicitors must contribute. Its purpose is to compensate members of the public who have suffered loss in certain circumstances resulting from solicitors' activities.

compensation order
> A court order made against a convicted criminal directing him to make amends to the person affected by his crime.

competency
> In relation to a witness, the state of being permitted to give admissable evidence.

complete specification

The main document in support of an application for a patent, which describes the invention, and what is new about it.

completion

A formal meeting between solicitors for the purchasers and vendors of property to hand over the purchase money and tie up the last formalities.

composition with creditors

An arrangement or settlement arrived at between a debtor and his creditors after bankruptcy proceedings have been started.

Comptroller and Auditor General

An official appointed by the Crown to examine accounts of income and expenditure made by the various Departments of State.

Comptroller-General

A government official in charge of patents, trade-marks, registered designs, copyright and related matters.

compulsory licence

A licence which the owner of a monopoly such as a patent or copyright is obliged by law in certain circumstances to grant to an applicant.

compulsory winding-up

A dissolution of a company brought about the order of the Court.

compurgation

A process in the Middle Ages of supporting a case by oath-helpers who would swear that a particular assertion was true.

concealment of birth

The statutory offence of disposing secretly of the body of a newly-born child.

concurrent sentence

A sentence of imprisonment expressed to run at the same time as a sentence for another offence, so that no additional time is served.

condemnation

The forfeiture of an article by due process of law, after it has been lawfully seized by an authorised person.

condition

An element in a contract of such fundamental importance that the agreement may fail if it is not carried out.

conditional bill of sale

A BILL OF SALE (q.v.) giving a claim over the goods or security for the payment of money, which ceases to have effect on repayment of the money.

conditional bond

A personal security for the payment of money or the carrying out of some other act, with a condition that it will become void if the act is completed within a certain time.

conditional discharge

An order made by a court in a criminal case, whereby no immediate punishment is imposed on the person discharged.

condition precedent

An event which must take place before a particular agreement can be carried out.

condition subsequent

A future event which may affect an agreement previously entered into.

condonation

In matrimonial law, the forgiving of misbehaviour on condition of good behaviour in the future. It was previously a bar to divorce.

conduct conducive to a breach of the peace

Threatening, abusive or insulting words, or writing, signs or visible matter intended or likely to cause a breach of the peace.

conference

In earlier times, a formal means of communication between representatives of both Houses of Parliament. Nowadays applied to a meeting between a junior barrister and his client.

confession

Generally applied to an admission of guilt made by someone to officers investigating a criminal offence.

confession and avoidance

In formal pleading of a case, an admission of the facts by the plaintiff, but joined with the raising of other facts which undermine (it is hoped) their effect.

confession statement

A formal admission of adultery made by husband or wife for the purpose of matrimonial proceedings.

confirmed letter of credit

An arrangement between a bank and its customer who has bought goods that payment will be made to the seller on presentation of certain documents of authority.

confusio *(Lat.)*

A mixture in which individual identification is impossible.

conjugal subjection

A defence available to a wife accused of a criminal offence, who can prove that her husband forced her to act as she did.

connivance

Intentional concurrence in the other spouse's adultery, which was formerly a bar to divorce.

conquest

In international law, the acquisition by one state of the territory of another by subjugating it completely, and declaring annexation of it.

consecutive sentence

A sentence of imprisonment expressed to run after a sentence imposed for another offence, so that the two terms are added together.

consensu *(Lat.)*

By agreement.

consensus ad idem *(Lat.)*

A situation where the thoughts of at least two people are in agreement.

consent

A defence that the plaintiff or victim acquiesced in the act complained of, which may be successfully raised in both civil and criminal cases.

consideration

The price or value by which one person obtains an undertaking in contract from another person.

consignee

The person who receives goods.

consignor

The person who despatches goods. In international trade, the last owner from whom imported goods are procured.

Consistory Court

An eccleiastical court now applying mainly to the clergy. One exists within each diocese in the land.

Consolidated Fund

Constituted in 1787 by combining the duties of Customs, Excise, Stamps and Post Office, and pledged for payment of the consolidated national debt of the United Kingdom.

consolidating statute

A statute which collects together all existing statutes on a particular subject without altering or amending any of the provisions in these statutes.

consolidation

The joining up of a number of legal issues which are in the course of proceedings in the same court.

consortium

(1) A legal euphemism for the pleasures of sexual relations,

the loss of which through injury may give rise to an action for damages.

(2) A pooling of effort by two or more business enterprises to achieve a particular objective, which will end when that objective is achieved.

conspiracy

(1) The agreement of two or more people to commit a criminal offence.

(2) A civil action in respect of the combination of people with the intention of causing damage to someone else, and which actually does some damage.

constable

Prior to the establishment of the police force, an official appointed in every parish to keep the peace.

constitutional law

The rules and conventions which make up the body of law, under which the sovereign powers of a country are exercised.

constructive desertion

Unreasonable behaviour on the part of one spouse which entitles the other spouse to stop cohabitation as man and wife.

constructive loss

The situation where the subject-matter of an insurance policy is justifiably abandoned, either because its destruction seems inevitable, or the cost of repair would be too great.

constructive malice

A doctrine formerly applied in murder cases to establish liability in situations where death occurred, although killing was not the prime purpose of the accused person.

constructive trust

A form of trust where a trustee performs an act in his own name in respect of property held by him as a trustee.

constructive warehousing

The formal recording of particulars of dutiable goods in a

BONDED WAREHOUSE (q.v.) without physically depositing them there.

consular invoice

A certificate given by a consul as to local prices and shipping charges for the purpose of import duties.

consultation

A meeting between a QUEEN'S COUNSEL (q.v.) and his clients.

consumer credit agreement

An agreement by which one person, the creditor, agrees to provide a consumer, the debtor, with credit up to a certain amount.

consumer credit business

Any business providing credit under REGULATED AGREEMENTS (q.v.) This is now illegal without an appropriate licence.

consumer hire agreement

A contract other than a hire-purchase agreement by which goods are transferred against the payment of specified sums by instalments.

consumer hire business

A business which makes goods available under a regulated consumer hire agreement.

consumer protection

Laws designed to protect the purchaser or user of goods or services against defects.

Consumer Protection Advisory Committee

A body created to advance the interests of fair trading, by considering whether any practice referred to it adversely affects a consumer's interests.

consummation of marriage

Sexual intercourse between husband and wife, which prevents nullity proceedings for failure to consummate the marriage.

contango

The act of postponing payment for shares from one settlement period until another.

contemnor *(Lat.)*

A person who has committed a contempt of court.

contempt of court

Disobedience of a court order, or an act interfering with the course of justice, or an act of disrespect to a court or judge.

contempt of Parliament

Any conduct bringing the authority of either House of Parliament into disrepute.

Continental Shelf

Much used in international and maritime law, it refers to the land area under the sea off the coast of a country, which extends in ledge form for a distance before eventually dropping away into deep sea.

contingent fee

An agreement by a lawyer to accept a case on the basis that he will be paid a proportion of any money recovered. Common in the United States, but contrary to professional rules in Britain.

contingent will

A will which takes effect only if a particular specified event takes place.

continuation clause

A clause in a policy of marine insurance automatically extending cover for 30 days, or until the ship's safe arrival, whichever is the earlier.

continuing guarantee

An arrangement by which the liability of the GUARANTOR (q.v.) is spread over a number of transactions covering a period of time.

contra *(Lat.)*

Contrary, in the sense of a differing decision in the reported cases, or a dissenting judgement.

contraband

Any article prohibited to be imported or exported, and therefore smuggled if the prohibition is evaded.

contra bonos mores *(Lat.)*
Against accepted good morals.

contract
A legally binding agreement under which one side promises to do or not to do certain things, at the request of the other side, or for its benefit.

contract for services
A contract for work to be carried out by an INDEPENDENT CONTRACTOR (q.v.), as opposed to a contract of service or employment.

contract of record
The entry of a debt on the official record of a COURT OF RECORD (q.v.), having the effect of a judgement imposed upon an individual.

contract of service
A contract of employment between master and servant (employer and employee).

contract under seal
A contract made by deed, otherwise known as a SPECIALTY CONTRACT (q.v.), and therefore not needing CONSIDERATION (q.v.).

contra proferentem *(Lat.)*
Against the person advancing a point contained in a particular document. Any ambiguity will be construed to such a person's disadvantage.

contribution clause
A clause in a fire insurance policy providing that if any other insurance has been taken out on the same property, the insurer under the later policy is only liable for a proportion of any loss.

contributory
A past or present shareholder in a company who is liable to it in a winding-up in respect of partly paid-up shares.

contributory negligence
Where the claimant in an action for negligence has been partly responsible for the damage caused by the defendant.

controlled tenant
A tenant of a property below a certain rateable value enjoying legal protection against rent increases imposed by his landlord. This type of tenancy was abolished in 1980.

convention
A practice which by custom is consistently followed, although not having the force of law.

conversion
(1) In EQUITY (q.v.) the doctrine that where property is directed ultimately to be converted into another form, eg into cash as result of a sale, that conversion is regarded as having already taken place.

(2) Any action by one person conflicting with the lawful ownership of goods by another person.

convertible banknotes
Notes which could be exchanged on demand for their face value in gold. No longer applicable to the banknotes of the United Kingdom.

convertible debentures
DEBENTURE CAPITAL (q.v.) giving the holders the right if they so desire of exchanging their debentures for shares.

conveyance
A document transferring a freehold interest in land after sale; the acts involved in drawing up the documentation.

conviction
A finding of guilt against an accused person in a criminal case.

co-operative
A trading organisation with a membership of equality of control, distributing any profits among the members.

copyright
> The right to control certain ways of dealing with a book, play, film, or other creative work which by law has been made the subject of protection. Protection is generally for the life of the creator, and a period after his death.

copyright collecting society
> A body responsible for the collection and distribution of royalties arising from the use of works protected by copyright.

copyright owner
> The person having the right to control any work protected by the system of COPYRIGHT (q.v.)

copyright piracy
> The unauthorised manufacture by copying of material protected by copyright, such as books, films and sound recordings.

coram judice *(Lat.)*
> In the presence of a judge.

coram non judice *(Lat.)*
> In the presence of someone not of judicial rank.

COREPER
> The Committee of Permanent Representatives of the Common Market.

co-respondent
> The man with whom a wife in matrimonial proceedings has committed adultery.

Corn Exchange
> A London market for dealing in grain and other crops for immediate as opposed to future delivery.

coroner
> An official, who should be legally or medically qualified, appointed to conduct enquiries by way of inquest into sudden death and TREASURE TROVE (q.v.)

coroner's court
> A court presided over by a coroner to conduct enquiries into cases of sudden death and TREASURE TROVE (q.v.)

coroner's jury
> A panel of not fewer than seven and not more than eleven persons summonsed to consider certain types of case where sudden death has taken place.

corporal punishment
> A former penalty of chastisement, now abolished.

corporate personality
> The legal condition of a company, which allows it to be treated as a person independent of its members; for example, it can be prosecuted and fined.

corporation aggregate
> A body consisting of a number of individual members, existing because of a charter or Act of Parliament.

corporation sole
> One of a number of offices which are capable of being filled only by one person at a time, for example, the Bishop of London.

corporation tax
> A tax paid by a company at a single rate on all profits, whether or not distributed.

corporeal chattels
> Material things, such as goods, which can be physically touched.

corpus *(Lat.)*
> Body.

corpus delicti *(Lat.)*
> The body involved in an unlawful killing.

corpus juris civilis *(Lat.)*
> An expression applied to the main principles of the codified law of ancient Rome.

costs between solicitor and own client
> The most generous basis on which costs are allowed, taking account of special fees and expenses.

Council of Europe
> A rather informal association of most of the non-Communist countries in Europe, co-operating in many fields, with the eventual aim of European unity.

Council of Legal Education
> The body controlling the syllabus and examinations for admission to the barrister's profession.

Council of Ministers
> The decision-making body of the E.E.C., which considers proposals put up by the COMMISSION (q.v.)

Council of the Stock Exchange
> The governing body of the Stock Exchange.

Council on Tribunals
> The governing body which reviews the constitution and operation of administrative tribunals.

count
> (1) A Parliamentary procedure to ascertain whether there are sufficient M.P.s present in the House of Commons to constitute a quorum.
>
> (2) An allegation of a criminal offence made formally in an INDICTMENT (q.v.)

counterclaim
> A cross-action brought by the defendant against the person claiming from him.

counterfeiting
> The act of making a false copy, particularly in relation to currency.

counterpart
> A duplicate copy of a legal document, particularly a lease.

countertrade
> In interantional trade, the system of paying for goods bought with other goods rather than with money.

country of origin
> The country in which goods are produced or manufactured.

county court
> The lowest level of court for civil disputes, such as contract, negligence, and landlord and tenant cases.

county court judge
> A member of the judiciary of circuit judge status, who sits in the county court to try civil matters.

county court registrar
> An official of the county court, subordinate to the judge, who performs administrative functions, and some lesser judicial duties.

county prosecuting solicitor (C.P.S.)
> A lawyer employed to conduct prosecutions for the police within the jurisdiction of a particular police prosecuting authority.

Court for Crown Cases Reserved
> A court which existed during the 19th century to decide difficult points of law arising during cases being tried in various other courts.

Court of Appeal (Civil Division)
> It hears appeals in civil cases from county courts, divisional courts, and the High Court itself.

Court of Appeal (Criminal Division)
> It hears appeals from the Crown Court in criminal cases triable by jury.

Court of Augmentations
> In the Middle Ages, a court hearing cases over the sale of Crown land subject to an annual rent.

Court of Chivalry
A court dating from feudal times, still with jurisdiction in matters relating to the use of coats of arms.

Court of Common Pleas
A court dealing with certain kinds of civil case, which lasted from the Middle Ages until 1873.

Court of Delegates
An appeal court for ecclesiastical and maritime matters, which was abolished in 1832.

Court of Ecclesiastical Causes Reserved
One of the surviving courts with jurisdiction in ecclesiastical cases to decide matters relating to the clergy.

Court of Exchequer
A court dealing principally with revenue matters, which continued from the Middle Ages until its abolition in 1873.

Court of Exchequer Chamber
A wide variety of appeals was heard by these courts, which were finally abolished in 1873.

Court of Faculties
An ecclesiastical court under the supervision of the Archbishop of Canterbury.

court of first instance
A general term for a court in which a case is first tried, from which an appeal to a higher court may be made.

Court of King's (or Queen's) Bench
A court which heard criminal appeals and a wide variety of civil cases from the 14th century until 1873.

Court of Piepowder
A medieval court exclusively for merchants, settling disputes arising in their market-places. The term probably derives from 'pieds poudrés'—dusty feet.

Court of Protection

A court which sits to administer the property of people who are of unsound mind, or under some other disability.

Court of Referees

A court of Parliament to determine disputes over private bills.

Court of Requests

Until the Civil War, a court associated with the Crown, which sought to assist poorer people who could not find a remedy at COMMON LAW (q.v.)

Court of Session

The supreme court of civil jurisdiction in the Scottish legal system; it should not be confused with the former English QUARTER SESSIONS (q.v.)

Court of Staple

A medieval commercial court held in one of the Staple towns, which enjoyed a monopoly of the most significant mercantile products.

Court of Star Chamber

A court of ancient origin, which achieved notoriety for its use of torture in criminal cases in the 16th century.

Court of Survey

A court which hears appeals by persons concerned with ships which have been found to be unseaworthy by the Department of Trade.

courts leet

Minor courts in medieval times having local jurisdiction under the supervision of the Lord of the Manor.

Courts Martial Appeal Court

A court staffed by High Court judges hearing appeals from courts-martial in the services.

Courts of the Staple

See Court of Staple.

covenant
>   An agreement, undertaking or promise contained in a deed.

coverture
>   Wedlock; the condition of matrimony.

cover note
>   A certificate containing particulars of temporary insurance cover arranged pending the issue of a full policy.

craft clause
>   A provision in a contract of marine insurance relating to the ferrying of goods in a transit craft to the vessel in which they will ultimately be conveyed.

credit brokerage business
>   Any commercial concern which puts potential customers in touch with organisations prepared to lend money under CONSUMER CREDIT AGREEMENTS (q.v.) It requires a licence from the Director-General of Fair Trading.

credit card
>   A document guaranteeing payment against a sales voucher countersigned by the holder of the card.

credit insurance company
>   A private insurance company guaranteeing the carrying out of contracts by overseas purchasers, where credit cannot otherwise be relied on.

credit note
>   A document issued by a seller for an item overcharged on an earlier invoice, or where goods delivered have to be taken back by him.

credit reference agency
>   Any concern furnishing information about a person's financial position. It needs a licence to operate from the Director-General of Fair Trading.

creditor's voluntary winding-up
>   A voluntary winding-up of a company without a statement

attached from the majority of directors that they consider that the company will be able to pay its debts in full.

creek

A tidal inlet which in the absence of special licence is not a lawful place of importation or exportation.

crime

A wrong against the community which is punishable by the state.

Criminal Appeal Reports

A series of case decisions in criminal matters of interest to specialist lawyers.

criminal bankruptcy

An order which may be made by a Crown Court on convicting someone whose offence caused loss or damage above a particular sum.

criminal conversation

An expression formerly used for adultery.

criminal damage

A criminal offence involving the deliberate causing of harm to goods or property.

Criminal Injuries Compensation Board

The body responsible for administering the scheme of compensating victims of violent crime.

Criminal Law Revision Committee

A body appointed to consider whether reform is necessary in areas of criminal law referred to it by the Home Secretary.

criminal libel

A serious defamation made in circumstances likely to provoke a breach of the peace, and therefore a criminal offence.

criminal responsibility

The age at which a person is regarded by the law as being capable of committing a criminal offence.

criminology

The scientific study of criminal motivation, its causes, effects and treatment.

cross-examination

Questioning put by an advocate to his opponent's witnesses in an attempt to weaken or contradict the other side's case.

cross-licensing

The situation where two or more companies grant licences to the other for the use of their own patents, usually where a common area of research is being explored.

Crown colony

A colonial territory not possessing an autonomous government of its own.

Crown copyright

The right of the Crown to control copyright in all works made by or under governmental directions.

Crown Court

The senior level of criminal court, which hears cases triable by jury.

Crown in Council

The reigning sovereign together with the Privy Council.

Crown Office Department

An office of the High Court which arranges the sequence of trials in the QUEEN'S BENCH DIVISION (q.v.)

Crown prerogative

The administration of justice exercised through the courts and judges on behalf of the sovereign.

Crown user

The right of the state to insist on the use of an invention otherwise protected by patent.

cruelty

Formerly a ground for divorce, now evidence of irretrievable breakdown of marriage.

crystallisation

The conversion of a FLOATING CHARGE (q.v.) over all the assets of a company into a FIXED CHARGE (q.v.) over definite assets. It takes place on the occurrence of certain events, such as a winding-up.

cucking-stool

An ancient form of punishment, on which a convicted person was ducked into unpleasant liquids.

culpa *(Lat.)*

Fault; blameworthiness.

cum testamento annexo *(Lat.)*

'With the will attached'. A GRANT OF ADMINISTRATION (q.v.) following the provisions of a will where no executor named is able or willing to act.

cumulative legacy

A gift by will of PERSONAL PROPERTY (q.v.) to the same person, in addition to a previous gift by the same will to the same person.

cumulative preference shares

A category of PREFERENCE SHARES (q.v.) in a limited company where any deficiency in paying previous dividends must be made up before paying ordinary shareholders.

curfew

A form of sentence which can be passed on a young offender by a criminal court, restricting his or her movements during the evening and night.

curia advisari vult (cur. adv. vult.) *(Lat.)*

The court wants time to reflect.

Curia Regis *(Lat.)*

The ancient council or court of the king, from which most of the chief courts of the present day flow either directly or indirectly.

currency

Generally applied to forms of money issued or circulated by

the governmental authority of a state, as opposed to a banker's draft.

custody

In matrimonial proceedings, a court order giving one parent the ultimate right to control the upbringing of a child, as opposed to a right of residence.

custom

A local rule both reasonable and certain, which is deemed to have existed since time immemorial, and which is accepted as part of the law of the land.

custom house

The public office at which the customs business of a port is carried out.

Customs and Excise Tariff

A volume prepared annually showing the duties, drawbacks and allowances of customs and excise.

customs bond

A security demanded by Customs and Excise for goods subject to a duty, which is not for the time being to be fully paid.

customs entry

A document in prescribed form giving particulars of goods from abroad which an importer wishes to pass through customs.

Custos Rotulorum *(Lat.)*

The chief representative of the Crown in each county, whose functions are now carried out by the Lord Lieutenant.

cy-près *(Fr.)*

A scheme directed by the court or the Charity Commissioners, so that the charitable intention of the donor or settlor of property can be given effect as nearly as possible where his wishes cannot be exactly carried out.

D

daily cause list
> A published list of cases to be heard in the High Court and Court of Appeal on a particular day.

damages
> An award made by way of compensation to the aggrieved party in a civil case.

damnosa hereditas *(Lat.)*
> An inheritance which turns out to be worthiess.

damnum *(Lat.)*
> Damage or loss.

damnum fatale *(Lat.)*
> Damage or loss brought about by fate rather than by anybody's personal responsibility.

damnum sine injuria *(Lat.)*
> Damage or injury which does not infringe a legal right, or give rise to a legal action.

dandy note
> A document in the Port of London to notify the delivery to the side of an exporting ship of goods from a warehouse.

dangerous drug
> A drug which, if listed in the relevant legislation, may be subject to a prohibition on importation.

date of commencement

The date at which an Act of Parliament or STATUTORY INSTRUMENT (q.v.) comes into effect.

day of grace

Until 1971, three days' grace, or relief from payment under a bill of exchange falling due on a fixed date, were allowed. Now abolished.

day training centre

Attendance as a condition of probation may be ordered at a centre for full-time non-residential training for offenders, to equip them more adequately for the demands of modern life.

dead freight

The sum due to a shipowner who is ready to fulfil a contract for the carriage of goods by sea, but where the charterer has failed to load a full cargo.

dear money

Money borrowed at a high rate of interest.

death by dangerous driving

The criminal offence of causing the death of another person by driving a vehicle in a manner regarded as dangerous by the road traffic legislation.

death grant

A state benefit payable to the next of kin, EXECUTOR (q.v.) or the person paying the funeral expenses of someone who dies.

death penalty

A sentence only at present passed in respect of treason or piracy.

de bene esse *(Lat.)*

Something allowed provisionally by a court, and subject to later confirmation.

debenture

Issued by a limited company in acknowledgement of a loan, generally secured on its assets. By contrast with DEBENTURE

STOCK (q.v.), it constitutes an individual debt between the company and the debenture holder.

debenture capital

Money borrowed on the security of the issue of DEBENTURES (q.v.) or DEBENTURE STOCK (q.v.), which is in effect a loan to a limited company against the security of its assets.

debenture stock

Issued by a company to raise a sum of money from a number of debenture stockholders, who all benefit from the security underlying the composite debt.

debit note

An additional invoice to cover an omission or undercharging on a previous invoice.

debitum in futuro solvendum *(Lat.)*

A debt falling due for payment at some time in the future.

debitum in praesenti *(Lat.)*

A debt currently due for payment.

de bonis asportatis *(Lat.)*

Relating to goods which have been taken away.

de bonis non administratis *(Lat.)*

Property left without administration (after death).

debt

A sum of money owed; an ancient form of action by which a claim could be made for money alleged to be owed.

debt collecting business

Any organisation which collects debts. It must be licensed by the Director-General of Fair Trading.

debt counselling business

Any concern advising clients on the liquidation of debts or the negotiation of settlements under consumer credit agreements. It must be licensed by the Director-General of Fair Trading.

deceit
>   A civil action in respect of a false statement made with intent that it should be acted on, and as a result of which, damage has been caused.

deck cargo
>   Cargo or stores carried in any uncovered space on the deck of a ship, or other covered place not forming part of the ship's registered tonnage.

declaration of association
>   A statement in the memorandum of association of a company that the subscribers wish to form a company, and that they agree to take the prescribed shares.

declaratory judgement
>   A PREROGATIVE ORDER (q.v.) made to restrain the Crown or any public authority from taking illegal action.

declaratory precedent
>   A decision of a court which is merely the application of an existing rule of law.

decree absolute
>   The final order made bringing a marriage to an end, three months after a DECREE NISI (q.v.)

decree nisi
>   An order made where a court is satisfied that a marriage should be dissolved, normally made absolute after three months.

de die in diem *(Lat.)*
>   From day to day.

deed of arrangement
>   A procedure by which a person in financial difficulties can put his property in trust for the benefit of his creditors, without actually becoming bankrupt.

Deemster
>   A judge of the Channel Islands or the Isle of Man.

de facto *(Lat.)*

As a matter of fact.

defamation

The wrongful lowering of a person's reputation in the minds of his fellow men.

defamatory statement

A statement lowering a person in the estimation of right-thinking members of society.

default action

An action to recover a debt or specific sum of money.

default summons

The form of summons for commencing a default action.

defeasance

Any collateral agreement relating to a BILL OF SALE (q.v.), which allows the bill to be set aside if events mentioned in the agreement take place.

defence

The side against which a civil claim is made or a crime alleged; a written statement setting out the facts on which the defendant in a civil case is going to rely.

defendant

In criminal law, a person subject to a criminal action; in civil law, a person against whom an action is brought.

defended divorce

A divorce case which, on a defence being lodged, must be transferred from the county court to the High Court.

deferred annuity

A policy by which payment of a stated annual sum, the annuity, is delayed for a specific number of years after the making of the contract.

deferred creditor

A creditor who has a low priority in participating in the division of any assets of a bankrupt.

deferred shares

A category of shares which may exist in the structure of a company, providing their holders with entitlement to all the remaining profit after the ordinary shareholders have received a fixed dividend.

de integro *(Lat.)*

Entirely; utterly; wholly.

de jure *(Lat.)*

As a matter of law.

delay defeats equity

The principle that EQUITY (q.v.) will not assist an injured or aggrieved person who has not taken steps to obtain redress in good time.

del credere agent

An agent who assumes responsibility for the accounts of his customers, and indemnifies his principal against losses caused by any customers introduced by him.

delegated legislation

Orders, regulations, and rules, all of which have the force of an Act of Parliament, but made by somebody outside Parliament to whom the power to make them has been deputed by Parliament.

delegatus non potest delegare *(Lat.)*

The principle that a person to whom certain functions have been delegated cannot himself delegate them. Thus a trustee may not, unless authorised, delegate to anyone else the performance of his duties.

delivered at frontier

A contract by which the seller agrees to deliver goods at a designated place at a particular frontier.

delivered domicile

A contract by which the seller must arrange to pay all charges for delivering goods to the buyer's premises.

delivery order

An order made by the owner of goods, allowing the person who has charge of them to hand them over to a specific person.

de minimis non curat lex *(Lat.)*

The principle that the law does not concern itself with trivialities.

demise charter

An agreement for the charter of a ship only, without its crew.

demise of the Crown

The passing of the Crown, on the death of the reigning king or queen, to his or her successor.

demonstrative bequest

The gift by will of money payable out of a specific fund.

demurrage

Money payable by charterers to a shipowner or transporter for delay to a vessel or truck due to her not being loaded or unloaded within an agreed period, or a reasonable period for loading and discharge.

demurrer

The plea by a person accused of a criminal offence that even if the facts alleged against him are correct, they do not amount to the offence charged.

de novo *(Lat.)*

From the beginning once again.

denaturing

The act of making a commodity unfit for human consumption by adding something to it.

deodand

From the Middle Ages until the mid-nineteenth century, applied to something either living or dead which had caused the death of a person, and was as a result liable to be forfeited.

Department of State
>An organ of central government headed by a Minister, popularly known as a Ministry. An example is the Department of the Environment.

Department of Trade Inspector
>A person who may be appointed by the Department of Trade to investigate the affairs of a company where there is a suggestion of serious mismanagement.

dependent domicile
>The DOMICILE (q.v.) of her husband which a wife formerly acquired on marriage.

dependent relative revocation
>A doctrine applied to nullify the act of revocation of a will, where the effect of the attempted revocation has been misunderstood by the person carrying it out.

deponent
>Someone who swears to a statement on oath.

deportation order
>An order requiring a person of non-United Kingdom nationality to leave this country, and to remain out of it.

deposition
>Oral statement of evidence taken down before magistrates at old-style committal proceedings.

deprivation of property order
>An order which can be made against a person convicted of certain crimes, depriving him of his rights in property used or intended for use in crime.

derelict
>An abandoned ship still afloat.

derogation
>The act of prejudicing, evading or completely destroying some entitlement or grant.

deserted wife's equity

A right of occupancy in the matrimonial home which a deserted wife enjoys, now a registrable interest.

desertion

(1) The continuing absence without leave of a member of the armed forces, seaman, or other person under an obligation to be present at a particular place at a particular time.

(2) In matrimonial law, the act of one spouse leaving the other, formerly a ground for divorce. Now evidence of irretrievable breakdown of marriage.

design law

A system of protecting industrial and manufactured designs, akin to and overlapping the copyright system.

detention centre

Designed for persons between 14 and 21, for periods up to six months where prison would be the only alternative.

deterrence

The theory that the punishment which a convicted criminal receives deters other people from committing similar offences.

deterrent sentence

A high sentence passed by a judge who has a choice of options, in order to make an example of the person he is sentencing.

detinue

The former name for the wrongful retention by one person of goods rightfully belonging to another.

devaluation

The lowering of the value of one state's currency against the currencies of other states. The official debasement of a currency.

devastavit *(Lat.)*

A charge against a PERSONAL REPRESENTATIVE (q.v.), for wasting the property of a dead person.

development

An act whereby an existing use of land or buildings is materially altered, so that planning permission must be obtained.

development land tax

A tax chargeable on the realised value of development, on the disposal of certain interests in land.

deviation

For purposes of marine insurance, the departure of a ship from a standard or agreed course.

devise

The giving of a freehold estate in land by legacy in a will.

devisee

The person to whom freehold estate such as houses and land is left by will.

dewarding

The process by which a child ceases to be a WARD OF COURT (q.v.), either by court order or by reaching full age.

dictum *(Lat.)*

Something said.

diffusion right

In copyright law, the right to relay works protected by copyright over cable systems (popularly known as 'cable TV').

dilatory motion

A procedural device in Parliament for temporarily delaying consideration of the motion currently before the House.

diminished responsibility

A defence to a charge of murder (reducing it to manslaughter), where it can be shown that a person suffered from such abnormality of mind that his mental responsibility was substantially impaired.

diplomatic immunity
The immunity from both civil and criminal proceedings granted to foreign ambassadors and certain categories of their staff.

direct evidence
The testimony of an eye-witness, or the production of a document amounting to the fact alleged. An example would be the production of a will, the existence of which had been denied by the other side.

directions
Orders given by a judge at a preliminary stage of a civil trial, which govern matters of procedure and presentation.

directive
An ordinance of the COUNCIL OF MINISTERS (q.v.) of the Common Market, which obliges member countries to achieve a certain result, without specifying the means.

directly applicable legislation
Laws made by the Common Market which take effect directly in this country, and do not need to be passed through Parliament.

Director of Public Prosecutions (D.P.P.)
A senior appointee in the Government Legal Service heading his own Department of lawyers. He advises certain other Government Departments, also the police in certain classes of case, and prosecutes in cases of particular difficulty or magnitude.

directors' report
A statement which must be attached each year to a company's balance sheet, relating to the company's affairs, its dividends and management.

disability
The legal condition of someone who is of unsound mind or under the age of eighteen.

disbarring
> The act of depriving a barrister of the right to practise, either as a disciplinary measure, or because the applicant wants to become a solicitor.

discharge
> The situation where the person who has made a promise in a contract becomes no longer bound by it.

discharge of bankruptcy
> A court order freeing a bankrupt from further claims against him, and allowing him to make a new start in life.

disclaimable property
> Property of a bankrupt subject to unfavourable conditions, which may be disclaimed by a TRUSTEE IN BANKRUPTCY (q.v.)

disclaimer
> The renunciation of a right to something.

discounting bills
> The purchase of bills of exchange at their face value, minus any interest remaining for the period before they mature.

discount market
> Collectively, those undertakings whose new business is dealing in sterling bills.

discovery
> The process of disclosure and inspection of documents prior to the trial of the main issue in a civil action.

disentailing and resettlement
> A means of keeping landed estates within a family by successively BARRING THE ENTAIL (q.v.), and resettling the property.

disgorging
> The act of removing sediment from effervescing wines in bottle.

dishonour

When a cheque is drawn on a particular bank, which declines to pay under it, that cheque is said to be dishonoured.

disqualification of directors

The provision for the vacation of office by directors of a company who have failed to fulfil certain conditions generally provided for in the articles of association.

dissentiente *(Lat.)*

Dissenting, particularly in relation to a legal agreement or the judgement of the court.

dissolution of marriage

The ending of the state of marriage between husband and wife, by DIVORCE (q.v.) or nullity.

dissolution of Parliament

The bringing to an end of a Parliament by exercise of the Royal Prerogative.

distillation test

The operation of measuring the original gravity of WASH (q.v.) or beer, or the alcoholic strength of wine and spirits.

distilling materials

Materials producing WORT (q.v.) or WASH (q.v.), the gravity of which can be ascertained by a SACCHAROMETER (q.v.)

distiller's warehouse

A warehouse provided by a distiller and approved for the deposit of distilled spirits under Crown control.

distinguishing

A technique used by judges to avoid following precedents set in earlier cases, by demonstrating that the cases differ from the case which they are currently hearing.

distrain

To seize goods, generally in satisfaction of unpaid rent, rates or taxes.

distress damage feasant

The right to seize and detain something causing damage while trespassing on land.

District Court Martial

The lowest level of court exercising jurisdiction under military law.

District Registrar

A judicial officer supervising a DISTRICT REGISTRY (q.v.), who decides interim issues and disputes arising during the course of certain legal proceedings.

District Registry

A branch office of the Central Office of the Supreme Court.

distringas *(Lat.)*

The authority to DISTRAIN (q.v.) in execution of a court order.

divided legal profession

The situation in England and Wales, and a few other English speaking countries, where the legal profession is split into two sections, barristers and solicitors.

division

The means by which a vote is taken in the House of Commons.

Divisional Court

Formed in the Queen's Bench, Chancery and Family Divisions of the High Court, to hear appeals from lower courts and tribunals.

divorce

An order bringing a marriage to an end.

Divorce Bar

The group of barristers specialising in proceedings relating to divorce, and connected matters such as custody of children and maintenance.

divorce county court

A COUNTY COURT (q.v.) with jurisdiction in matrimonial matters.

divorce petition

A formal statement by husband or wife seeking a divorce, which sets out the details of the marriage, and the reasons for seeking the relief claimed.

Divorce Registry

The Principal Registry of the Family Division of the High Court, situated in London.

dockage

Berthing dues payable by a vessel which has used acommodation while taking on cargo.

dock brief

Formerly available to a person accused of a criminal offence triable by jury, who from the dock could select any barrister in robes sitting in court, who was obliged to defend him for the sum of £2 6s. 8d.

dock warrant

A warrant issued by a harbour authority allowing a particular person to take possession of goods.

Doctors Commons

An order of advocates specialising in Roman law, which was abolished in the 19th century.

doctrine of the Seals

The principle that acts of the EXECUTIVE (q.v.) to which the Crown is a party must be carried out by Order in Council, the Great Seal, or under the Sign Manual.

documentary bill

A bill of exchange attached to the bill of lading, insurance policy and invoice for the goods with which it is connected.

domestic proceedings

Court business dealing with relations between people living together as man and wife, and their offspring.

domestic tribunal

A body applying the rules of a professional or other grouping, for example the Disciplinary Tribunal of the Law Society.

domicile
> The country in which an individual is considered to be 'at home' or permanently resident because of his long connection with it.

domicile of choice
> The DOMICILE (q.v.) which a person has chosen in substitution for his DOMICILE OF ORIGIN (q.v.), and shown by his intention to remain there (the ANIMUS MANENDI (q.v.)).

domicile of origin
> The DOMICILE (q.v.) which a person takes from one of his parents at birth. A legitimate person assumes the domicile of his father, an illegitimate person that of his mother.

dominant tenement
> Land benefiting from an easement or PROFIT À PRENDRE (q.v.)

dominium *(Lat.)*
> The right of ownership.

donatio mortis causa *(Lat.)*
> A gift made in contemplation (anticipation) of death.

double insurance
> Over-insurance by taking out two or more policies in respect of the same risk, in excess of the total to be indemnified.

double probate
> A grant of probate made to a person who, being one of more than four executors, has applied for a vacancy which has occurred.

doublings
> Spirits of the second extraction.

dramming
> An allowance of duty-free spirit for consumption given by distillers to their workmen under the supervision of the Distillery Officer until 1899, when it was forbidden.

draught of a ship
> The depth of water necessary to float a ship.

drawback

The repayment in certain circumstances of duty paid on goods which have been re-exported or shipped as ship's stores.

drawee

The person on whom a call to pay is made by a written instrument, for example a bank; the bank on which a cheque is drawn.

drawer

A person who has drafted or written something out, often used in the context of cheques and other negotiable instruments; the person signing a cheque.

drawings

Technical illustrations which accompany an application for a patent.

droit de suite *(Fr.)*

A right claimed by painters and other artists to share in any increased value on subsequent sales of their works. Not recognised in Britain.

droit moral *(Fr.)*

The right of an author or other creative worker to protect his reputation. Recognised by international convention, but not fully accepted in Britain.

droits of admiralty

Goods afloat at sea above the low water mark, but which have not become WRECKAGE (q.v.) by touching bottom.

dropped order

The means by which an item of Parliamentary business is not proceeded with, and is therefore dropped from the order paper.

drunken driving

A popular expression for the criminal offence of driving a motor vehicle with more than the prescribed amount of alcohol in the blood, or breath.

duress
> Pressure brought to bear to influence a person's decision.

dubitante *(Lat.)*
> Expressing scepticism about the accuracy of a legal argument or decision.

dumping
> The exporting of a product at a price which is below the cost of production, or the price on the home market, or otherwise unfairly subsidised.

dum sola et casta *(Lat.)*
> 'While single and chaste'. A reservation sometimes made in a husband's financial provision for a wife, terminating the arrangement if she remarried or committed adultery, according to the circumstances.

durante minore aetate *(Lat.)*
> During the infancy of an executor.

duty of care
> An element which must be shown to exist between two people before one can bring an action against the other for negligence.

duty paid goods
> Goods in respect of which the Commissioners of Customs and Excise are satisfied that all relevant duties have been paid.

E

Early Day Motion

A Parliamentary motion for which no particular time has been fixed, but for which it is hoped to obtain time at an early date.

easement

The right to make limited use of another person's land, as in a right of way.

East India Company

Chartered in 1660 with exclusive trading rights in all places east of a line from the Cape of Good Hope to the Straits of Magellan.

ecclesiastical court

A court applying the canon law of the Church from medieval times, and exercising some lay jurisdiction. Now only concerned with matters relating exclusively to the Church.

Economic and Social Committee of the E.E.C.

A consultative body of the Common Market, which considers proposals suggested by the COMMISSION (q.v.) and the COUNCIL OF MINISTERS (q.v.)

Economic and Social Council of the U.N.

A committee of the General Assembly of the UNITED NATIONS (q.v.), responsible for the promotion of economic and social progress.

Economic Commission for Europe

One of the regional economic commissions established by the United Nations to supervise a variety of social and economic matters.

egg-shell skull

A term for the principle that a person who injures someone else must take him as he finds him, and be responsible for any extra damage due to his special peculiarities.

ejectment

A civil action for the recovery of land where a person has been wrongfully dispossessed.

ejusdem generis *(Lat.)*

A rule of interpretation for Acts of Parliament and documents which means that where specific words are followed by general words, the general words cannot have a wider meaning than the specific words.

election

Choice. A doctrine by which the person to whom a gift by will has been made, and part of whose property has mistakenly been willed by the dead person to someone else, can choose which property he wishes to keep.

embezzlement

A former crime involving obtaining by fraud, now replaced by the law relating to THEFT (q.v.)

embracery

An ancient term for the offence of corrupting a juror.

Employment Appeal Tribunal

Hears appeals on points of law from industrial tribunals.

employment rehabilitation allowance

A non-contributory state benefit payable to people who have been sick or injured, or who are in someway handicapped, and who are taking a rehabilitation course.

enabling legislation

An Act of Parliament giving authority to a Minister or body to make regulations putting general principles into detailed effect.

enacting words

A form of words appearing on a Bill in Parliament immediately following the title and any preamble.

endorsement

(1) A signature, literally 'on the back of' a document, often in the context of making a transfer.

(2) Recording of traffic convictions on a driving licence.

endowment assurance policy

A policy of ASSURANCE (q.v.), by which it is agreed that payment will be made either after expiry of a fixed term, or on the death of the life assured, if earlier.

enforcement of judgement

The means of obtaining payment from a person against whom a court order has been made.

enfranchise

To grant a liberty to someone, particularly that of voting in elections.

English Reports

A collection of all the private series of reports of cases made up to 1865, when an official system was established.

engrossment

The preparation of a formal legal document in its final form, ready for completion by swearing, signing or other formality.

enlargement of title

An extension of a time limit.

entail

A grant of land to a person with subsequent transfer limited to his heirs was said to be entailed. No longer possible in England since 1925.

enticement
> A right of civil action which a husband formerly had against someone who had enticed his wife away from him.

entry for trial
> The procedure by which the person making a claim must set the case down for trial, or risk it being dismissed for want of prosecution.

entry of appearance
> The official notice given by a person against whom a civil claim has been made, to the effect that he intends to defend the matter.

en ventre sa mère *(Fr.)*
> An unborn child, who may in certain circumstances enjoy legal rights.

e. & o.e. (errors and omissions excepted)
> A reservation of the right, generally on an invoice, to correct later any errors or ommissions which may become apparent.

eo instanti *(Lat.)*
> At that moment.

equality is equity
> The principle that EQUITY (q.v.) will find that property is held jointly, where two or more people have contributed to it, although it is only held in the name of one of them.

Equal Opportunities Commission
> An official body set up to promote equality of opportunity between men and women, and to work for the elimation of discrimination.

equitable execution
> A form of action to enforce a court order where the judgement

debtor has property or interests which cannot be reached by normal legal processes.

equitable interest

A supplementary form of right developed by the Chancellor's system of EQUITY (q.v.) Though weaker than a legal right developed from the common law, it supplements that system. An example would be a trust.

equitable lien

A right over property bestowed by law on someone who is not at the time the owner of the property. An example would be an unpaid seller of land who had transferred legal title to the purchaser.

equitable mortgage

The tendering of land as security for a loan, so that an equitable interest in that land is established in favour of the lender.

equitable mortgage of shares

The deposit of share certificates with a lender as security for a loan, creating merely an equitable title without transfer or registration.

equitable order

A procedure against a JUDGEMENT DEBTOR (q.v.) who has an interest in land which cannot be taken in satisfaction of the debt.

equity

Fairness or natural justice. Until 1873 a separate system of law administered by the Court of Chancery, designed to mitigate the harshness of the old common law, it now applies in all courts.

equity acts in personam

The principle in EQUITY (q.v.) that a court can act against a person in a dispute, by committing him, rather than against the property which is in dispute.

equity follows the law
>   The principle that EQUITY (q.v.) follows on behind the COMMON LAW (q.v.)

equity leans against double portions
>   The principle that where a parent, having already made provision for a child by way of a PORTION (q.v.), subsequently makes similar provision for the same child, the second provision will be taken to be in substitution for the first.

equity looks on that as done which ought to have been done
>   The principle that EQUITY (q.v.) will regard a formality as having been carried out if it appears fair to do so.

equity looks to the intent rather than to the form
>   The principle that EQUITY (q.v.) tries to do justice by applying the intention of the parties rather than the strict letter of what was actually written.

equity of redemption
>   The right of a mortgager to have his property revested in him free from restriction on payment of the debt, interest and costs.

equity share capital
>   The section of the ISSUED CAPITAL (q.v.) of a limited company, usually its ordinary shares, which places no restriction on the holders to participate in dividends or capital distributions.

equity will not suffer a wrong to be without a remedy
>   The principle that no wrong which is capable of being righted should remain unrighted.

escheat
>   Until the 19th century, the forfeiture of his land by a tenant who had been found guilty of a serious crime.

escrow
>   A deed delivered subject to a condition to be fulfilled later.

established church
>   The church accepted by a particular state as the one truly teaching a particular faith, and therefore accorded certain privileges.

established civil servant

A person serving in an established capacity in the permanent service of the Crown, as opposed to one who is temporarily employed or on probation.

estate bill

A Bill brought before Parliament to allow some form of landed interest to be dealt with in a way other than that considered in any will or testamentary document.

estimate

An offer, generally in writing, to carry out certain work at a stated price.

estimates of expenditure

Annual estimates of expenditure prepared for the Treasury by the Ministers responsible for the armed forces and the civil service.

estoppel

A rule of evidence that a person cannot deny the existence of a particular state of affairs which he has himself brought about, and on the basis of which another person has acted.

estoppel as to payment

The principle that a limited company cannot subsequently claim any payment in respect of shares which have been stated on the share certificate to be fully paid up.

estoppel by conduct

The principle by which a person who has led another person to believe that a particular situation exists is not able to escape the consequences of his conduct.

estoppel by deed

The refutation of another person's denial of particular facts, by pointing to the contents of a deed.

estoppel by record

The refutation of a person's denial of a particular state of affairs, by pointing to the judgement of a court.

estreat
> To obtain a copy of a Court record of bail or a fine.

estreated
> The term applied to the personal security for the attendance of a witness (recognizance) which has become forfeit due to non-attendance.

esturial traffic
> Water trade within defined limits of the Thames, Mersey, Clyde, Forth, Tyne and Humber estuaries, deemed not to be trade by sea.

et seq (et sequentes) *(Lat.)*
> In relation to a reference in a book, 'and in the following pages.'

Eurocrat
> A popular expression for an international civil servant employed by one of the institutions of the Common Market.

Eurodollars
> Dollar balances held in European banks by companies or individual account holders.

European Atomic Energy Community (Euratom)
> One of the organisations making up the European Economic Community (or Common Market).

European Coal and Steel Community (E.C.S.C.)
> One of the organisations comprising the European Community, or Common Market.

European Court of Justice
> The legal forum of the Common Market, the final interpreter and enforcer of E.E.C. legislation.

European Development Fund
> The means by which the Common Market's schemes of assistance for less developed countries are put into effect.

European Economic Community (E.E.C.)
> The Common Market, established by the Treaty of Rome.

European Free Trade Area (EFTA)

An association including Austria, Iceland, Norway, Portugal, Sweden and Switzerland existing to promote free trade in industrial products. The United Kingdom left in 1972 on joining the Common Market, which itself has free trade agreements with the EFTA states.

European Investment Bank

An organ of the Common Market arranging financial assistance for matters in which the E.E.C. is concerned, and for certain under-developed regions.

European Monetary Co-operation Fund

A reserve fund of the central banks of the Common Market countries.

European Parliament

An assembly of delegates from the member-states of the Common Market, who sit under party affiliation to consider E.E.C. policy.

European Space Agency

An organisation of Western European states for the co-ordination of research and execution of developments in space.

euthanasia

A term applied to the taking of the life of another person in order to put an end to their suffering. Also known as mercy killing, it is not at present a defence to a criminal charge.

evidence

The proof by which facts alleged in a case can be substantiated.

ex abundanti cautela *(Lat.)*

Indicating the exercise of a good deal of caution. Literally, 'from an abundance of caution.'

ex aequo et bono *(Lat.)*

In accordance with justice and fairness.

Examiner of the Court

A person appointed by the court to take evidence on oath from a witness who is otherwise unable to attend court.

examination in chief

The taking of oral evidence from one of his own witnesses by an advocate in court.

excepted persons

An expression used in contracts of insurance to indicate classes of work and accident to which cover will not be given.

exceptional depravity

Serious matrimonial misconduct allowing the other spouse to petition for divorce inside the normal time-limits.

excess of jurisdiction

Applied to situations where a person acting as a judge or magistrate has exceeded his powers.

excess vote

The subsequent authorisation by Parliament of an excessive amount spent by a public body.

exchange control

A system to control the movement of its currency outside a country. At present abolished in the U.K.

exclusive licence

A contract granting the licensee the sole right to exercise whatever is granted under the licence, to the exclusion of everyone else.

Exchequer Bill

A government security in the form of a promissory note having a life of 5 years and bearing interest at six monthly intervals. It was superseded by the TREASURY BILL (q.v.) in 1897.

ex contractu *(Lat.)*

Arising from the contract.

ex debitato justitiae *(Lat.)*
Something rightfully due.

ex delicto *(Lat.)*
Connected with a tort or civil wrongdoing.

ex dividend
Applied to shares which are sold on the basis that the purchaser does not receive the benefit of any dividend which is in the process of being paid.

executed
Something which has been carried out, particularly the terms of a contract.

executed consideration
Something wholly performed by one party to a contract immediately an agreement is made, as part of the contractual quid pro quo, such as a payment in advance.

execution creditor
A person owed a debt by a company in liquidation, who has attempted to obtain it independently by attachment or execution.

execution of a will
The making of a valid will by writing, signing and ATTESTING (q.v.)

execution of process
The procedure whereby bailiffs are ordered to take the property of a person against whom judgement has been given, to the value of any amount for which he is liable, and which has not already been paid over.

Executive
The body which administers the laws passed by Parliament. It is made up principally of Departments of State, which are headed by Ministers.

executive director

Generally a full-time member of the board of a company, with responsibility for the work of a particular division of its activity.

executor

A person appointed under a will, responsible for administering a dead person's estate and distributing it according to the terms of the will.

executor according to the tenor

An EXECUTOR (q.v.) appointed by implication, and not in specific terms by the will itself.

executor de son tort

A person who has become an EXECUTOR (q.v.) by wrongful means or by interference.

executory

The state of not being completed, particularly relating to a contract.

executory consideration

A contractual promise to confer a benefit or suffer a detriment at some time in the future, as part of the contractual quid pro quo.

exemplary damages

A high award of damages made to underline what is seen as a bad case.

exempt agreement

For the purpose of consumer credit legislation, an agreement which is not a REGULATED AGREEMENT (q.v.)

exempted business

Parliamentary business introduced at certain times which is exempted from interruption.

exempt supply

A supply of goods or services for the purposes of VALUE ADDED TAX (q.v.), which is exempt from any charge to the tax.

ex facie *(Lat.)*
> Apparently; as it seems.

ex gratia *(Lat.)*
> As a favour (and not as a right).

ex hypothesi *(Lat.)*
> As is self-evident; as is assumed.

ex nudo pacto non oritur actio *(Lat.)*
> No action at law can be based on a bare promise.

ex pacto illicito non oritur actio *(Lat.)*
> No case can be based on an illegal agreement.

ex parte *(Lat.)*
> A proceeding or step in a case taken by one side in the absence of the other side.

expert witness
> A witness with specialised knowledge of a particular situation, who may give in evidence his opinion on technical matters.

Expiring Laws Continuance Bill
> An annual Bill passed by Parliament so that certain temporary measures which would otherwise die out can continue.

explanatory memoradum
> A note attached to a Bill introduced in Parliament to explain what it is hoped it will achieve.

Export Credits Guarantee Department (E.C.G.D.)
> An organisation designed to help exporters by providing insurance against the risk that buyers abroad might prove insolvent or be prevented from meeting their obligations.

export entry
> A shipping bill for goods which must be pre-entered before export; in the case of other goods for export, their particulars in prescribed form.

export licence
> A permit to export a particular article, the sending of which abroad would otherwise be prohibited or restricted.

ex post facto *(Lat.)*
> Subsequent to a main event.

express malice
> In relation to murder, the intention to kill.

expressio unius est exclusio alterius *(Lat.)*
> A rule of interpreting Acts of Parliament which provides that if specific words expressed in an Act are not followed by general words, that Act will only be applied to things expressly mentioned.

expressum facit cessare tacitum *(Lat.)*
> A principle of interpreting contracts, so that if one matter is expressly stated, that prevents any other interpretation being implied.

ex quay: duties on buyer's account
> A contract by which the seller agrees to deliver goods to the buyer at the quay or wharf at a designated port, the buyer to meet import duties and customs charges.

ex quay: duty paid
> A contract by which the seller agrees to deliver the goods to the quay or wharf at a designated port, and to meet all import duties and customs charges.

ex ship
> A contract by which the seller undertakes to place goods at the buyer's disposal on board a particular ship at the usual unloading point in a designated port.

extortionate credit bargain
> Any consumer CREDIT AGREEMENT (q.v.) which is grossly extortionate, or which contravenes normal principles of fair dealing.

ex toto *(Lat.)*
> Absolutely.

extradition

A system of reciprocal treaties between countries regulating the handing over of people accused of particular crimes in another country.

extraordinary meeting

A meeting of the company, not being either the STATUTORY MEETING (q.v.), or the ANNUAL GENERAL MEETING (q.v.), for the purpose of carrying out some special or urgent business.

extraordinary resolution

A decision passed by at least three-quarters of the members of a company present and voting at a GENERAL MEETING (q.v.), where notice to propose the matter as an extraordinary resolution has been given.

ex turpi causa non oritur actio *(Lat.)*

The principle that a legal action may not be founded on an unlawful or immoral business.

ex works contract

An agreement by which the seller makes the goods available for collection by or on behalf of the buyer at the place of manufacture or some other specified location.

F

faciendum *(Lat.)*
> Something still to be carried out.

fact
> In jury trials, matters of fact in general are for the jury to decide, as opposed to questions of law, which should be left to the judge.

factor
> An agent who in the ordinary course of his business has authority to buy or sell goods, or to raise money on the security of goods.

facultative re-insurance
> The precaution taken by insurers of spreading their risks and farming out their less attractive policies.

Faculty of Advocates
> The body governing the senior branch of the legal profession in Scotland, the advocates being equivalent to the barristers of England and Wales.

failure to consummate
> An allegation seeking to establish NULLITY (q.v.) in matrimonial proceedings, by claiming that sexual relations between the parties never took place.

fair comment

A defence to an action for defamation whereby the words complained of are shown by the defence to be in the public interest.

fair dealing

In relation to a copyright work, the limited right to quote from it without permission for such matters as criticism, review and reporting.

falsa demonstratio non nocet *(Lat.)*

A false description does not nullify. (This principle referred to advertising claims where there was no fraud, but must today be considered in the light of consumer protection laws.)

false attribution of authorship

A right of action in copyright law against someone who falsely claims that his own work is someone else's or who without permission puts someone else's name on his own work as author.

false imprisonment

(1) A cause of action to compensate a person who has been wrongfully detained.

(2) The crime of restraining another person's liberty without lawful justification.

false representation

A false statement deliberately made.

falsification of accounts

The criminal offence of destroying, falsifying or concealing any document or record.

Family Division

The section of the High Court dealing chiefly with matrimonial matters, and arrangements between parent and child.

family income supplement

A state benefit payable to people bringing-up children on low earnings from full-time work.

family law

The area of law governing the rights, duties and status of husband and wife, parent and child, and other members of a household.

family provision

Legislation ordering reasonable provision for certain dependent relatives to be made out of a dead person's estate, where this would not otherwise be effective.

farmer of the revenue

A person to whom the right of levying duties of customs and of excise was let for a particular period. The practice finally ceased in 1683.

f.a.s. (free alongside ship)

A contract by which the seller undertakes to deliver goods alongside a nominated ship at its loading berth in a specified port.

Father of the House

The senior member of the House of Commons, by virtue of having sat for the longest unbroken period.

f.c. & s. (free of capture and seizure)

A clause in a policy of marine insurance excluding loss by capture and seizure of the ship and/or the goods.

feature music

Music on a film soundtrack intended to be heard by the actors, which attracts copyright royalties at a higher rate than BACKGROUND MUSIC (q.v.)

federal state

A union of states in which control of external relations for all of them has been permanently given up to a central government.

fee simple absolute

A freehold interest, equivalent to absolute ownership.

feints

The impure part of a distillation.

felony

At one time, a classification of serious crimes, which has now been abolished.

female servant duty

A tax levied in 1785 on anyone employing a female servant. It increased in proportion to the number employed, but was abolished in 1792.

feme couverte *(Fr.)*

A married woman.

feme sole *(Fr.)*

An unmarried or single woman, whose rights in law were at one time very different from those of a married woman.

ferae naturae *(Lat.)*

An expression applied to animals of a dangerous species, or those not commonly domesticated in Britain.

feudal tenure

Medieval system of land holding introduced to England and Wales by the Normans.

fiat *(Lat.)*

A consent. Used for the bringing of a prosecution with the consent of the Attorney-General.

fidelity insurance

A form of insurance policy to protect employers from loss by,fraud on the part of specified employees handling cash on their behalf.

fiduciary capacity

The capacity under which someone holds property in trust for another person.

F.G.A. (foreign general average)

In marine insurance, an acknowledgement by UNDERWRITERS (q.v.) that they will abide by foreign law in the event of a GENERAL AVERAGE loss (q.v.)

Field General Court Martial
> A court exercising jurisdiction under military law, either overseas or on active service, and generally in more serious cases.

fieri facias (fi. fa.) *(Lat.)*
> A writ obtained for the purpose of seizing a judgement debtor's money and selling his goods.

filing certificate
> The receipt given by the Patent Office for an application for a patent.

filius adulterinus *(Lat.)*
> The child of an adulterous relationship.

filius nullius *(Lat.)*
> An illegitimate child.

final dividend
> Any distribution made by a company at the end of its financial year, from which is deducted any payment on account made by way of interim dividend.

financial provision
> In matrimonial proceedings, a general expression for the financial support which one spouse must make for the other.

fine
> A financial punishment imposed by a court in respect of a crime.

finings
> Substances used for the clarification of beer.

firearms certificate
> A licence granted by the police authority for the district in which the applicant resides, authorising the possession of a firearm and ammunition.

firm
> A term applied to a business carried on as a partnership, usually to distinguish it from a limited company.

firm underwriting
>An agreement by a person underwriting an issue of shares in a company that he will take the shares in any event, and not simply if they remain unsold to the public.

first and paramount lien
>The LIEN (q.v.) which a company may hold over the shares of one of its members who owes it money.

first class paper
>Payable orders drawn on financial institutions of the highest reputation.

fishes royal
>Sturgeon, porpoises, whales and dolphins, which if caught within territorial waters or stranded belong to the Crown.

Fishing Boat Register
>A register of all British sea fishing boats operating from a United Kingdom port, controlled by the REGISTRAR OF SHIPPING (q.v.)

fixed assets
>That part of the property of a company which it is intended to retain for use in the business—land, buildings, equipment etc.

fixed charge
>Security for a loan given in the form of a charge over certain definite and identifiable assets.

fixed sum credit
>A loan for a specified sum of money, as opposed to a loan up to a certain limit.

flag discrimination
>Special treatment in some matter such as crewing or placing contracts given to the subjects of particular states.

fleet policy
>An insurance policy by which several vessels or vehicles belonging to one owner are covered by the same agreement.

floating charge

Security for a loan given over the assets of a person or company in general, and not fixed on certain definite items.

floating policy

A policy of marine insurance describing the contract in general terms, but leaving the name of the ship and other particulars to be inserted later.

flotation

The establishment of a company as a going concern financially.

flotsam

Cargo jettisoned from a ship which floats upon the surface of the sea, or wreckage staying on the surface of water.

f.o.b. (free on board)

A contract by which the seller must deliver the goods without further charge on board ship in a specified port.

f.o.b. airport

A contract by which the seller agrees to deliver goods into the care of a particular air carrier at a specified departure airport.

following the trust property

The right of recovering trust property from someone not entitled to obtain it, who has not acted in good faith.

Food and Agriculture Organisation (F.A.O.)

One of the specialised agencies of the UNITED NATIONS (q.v.), responsible for the development of world agricultural resources.

f.o.r. (free on rail)

A contract by which the seller undertakes to load goods onto a specified railway as freight, for a destination nominated by the buyer.

forbearance to sue

A promise not to enforce a legal right.

force majeure *(Fr.)*

Irresistible force, making the carrying out of a particular act or event impossible.

forcible entry

An ancient criminal offence of taking possession of land, violently and without authority.

foreclosure

The transfer of the whole of a borrower's interest in mortgaged property to the lender, after the borrower has not complied with a court order requiring repayment.

foreign enlistment

A criminal offence constituted by a citizen of the United Kingdom joining the forces of a nation at war with another nation friendly to the United Kingdom.

foreign going ship

A ship trading between a foreign country and the United Kingdom, Channel Islands or the Isle of Man.

foreign port

A port situated outside the United Kingdom, Channel Islands or the Isle of Man.

forensic medicine

Medical knowledge related to legal matters.

forensic science

Scientific knowledge related to legal matters.

foreshot

The first running-off of a spirit from a distillation.

forfeiture of shares

The automatic loss of shares by a shareholder who has failed to respond to a CALL ON SHARES (q.v.)

forgery

The making of a false document in order that it may be used as genuine.

form
> The formalities of a SPECIALTY CONTRACT (q.v.) as opposed to a simple contract.

forms of action
> The only procedures by which civil cases could formerly be started in the courts, latterly modified, and finally abolished in the 19th century.

fornication
> Sexual intercourse outside the bounds of marriage. It may be either gratuitous or paid for.

forthwith
> As soon as practical in the circumstances of a particular case.

forwarder's certificate of shipment
> Documentary evidence that shipment has been carried out on a specified vessel.

f.o.t. (free on truck)
> A contract by which the seller agrees to load goods onto a suitable road transport vehicle for a destination selected by the buyer.

founder's shares
> A class of shares in a limited company generally sharing in profits after the payment of any dividend on ordinary shares.

f.p.a. (free of particular average) clause
> A clause in a policy of marine insurance exempting underwriters from responsibility except for GENERAL AVERAGE (q.v.) or for loss from stranding, burning or sinking.

frankpledge
> An ancient form of policing various communities.

fraud
> Conduct based on deceit, forgery or corruption.

fraudulent conveyance
> For the purposes of bankruptcy, a transfer of property in order to defeat a creditor.

fraudulent misrepresentation

An untrue statement of fact, made with knowledge of its falsity, or without belief in its truth, or without caring whether it is true or false.

fraudulent preference

A transfer of property made to defeat a creditor, amounting to an ACT OF BANKRUPTCY (q.v.)

freeboard deck

The deck shown by the deck-line mark on a ship's side.

free circulation

For the purposes of the import/export trade, goods which have paid duty on importation to the United Kingdom, or which were produced here. Goods may now be in free circulation within the EEC.

freedom of testamentary succession

The freedom which formerly existed to cut one's close relatives off 'with a shilling' in one's will, which now is no longer possible.

free entry

A form of customs entry required to be completed by the importer for goods which are free of duty.

freehold

The right of absolute ownership in land.

free in and out

In ships' charters, an expression denoting that the shipowner is responsible for all charges except unloading, loading and dry-dock.

free movement of capital

One of the basic aims of the Common Market, which is to get rid of restrictions on the movement of finance between people living in the various member countries.

free of capture and seizure

A clause in a policy of insurance by which the risks of war are excluded.

free of charges

A contract by which the seller of goods includes all delivery charges to a named destination in his price.

free on board value

The amount to be shown by the exporter in customs documentation as the value of goods being exported.

free pardon

Part of the Royal Prerogative, by which both conviction and sentence are remitted.

free port

An area in which goods may be landed, stored, mixed, blended, repacked, manufactured and reshipped without customs intervention.

free tenant

A tenant of licensed premises who is under no obligation to obtain his alcoholic drink from a particular source.

free use

A limited form of dealing with a work otherwise subject to copyright protection, which does not require the consent of the copyright owner.

freight

A sum of money paid for the carriage of goods, usually by sea under a contract of AFFREIGHTMENT (q.v.)

freight account

A bill sent by the shipowner to the consignor of goods for the cost of carrying them to their destination.

freight forwarder

Someone acting on behalf of an exporter in the shipping, insurance and documentation of goods.

freight or carriage paid

A contract by which the seller undertakes to send the goods at his own expense to a named destination.

freight pro rata

The entitlement of a shipowner under a contract for the carriage of goods by sea to a proportionate payment where only part of the contract has been fulfilled.

freight release

An instruction from a shipping company to a dock superintendant, instructing him to deliver goods to a particular person.

frolic of his own

A doctrine of civil law exempting an employer from liability for damage caused by an employee acting outside the course of his employment.

front bench

The benches in the House of Commons where Ministers of the governing party and the senior members of the opposition sit.

fructus industriales *(Lat.)*

Products of cultivation; agricultural or horticultural products.

fructus naturales *(Lat.)*

Wild vegetation.

frustration

The situation where it becomes impossible to carry out a contract.

full title

The official title of an Act of Parliament, with a short description of its object.

fully paid-up shares

Company shares on which the whole amount of the nominal value has been paid.

functus officio *(Lat.)*

No longer enjoying any power or authority in a matter, having discharged one's responsibility.

funds

A term applied to money paid or brought into court.

future goods

Goods which are to be manufactured or acquired by the seller after the contract has been made.

futures market

A market dealing in crops or commodities not immediately available for delivery.

G

gaming contract

A promise to give something to another person on the ascertainment of the result of a game.

gaming machine licence duty

A tax payable by the operators of certain categories of gaming machine.

garnishee order

An order forcing a third person who owes money to a judgement debtor to pay it to the judgement creditor instead.

gavelkind

A system of land holding or tenure, formerly prevalent in Kent and certain parts of London.

gazetting

The act of giving notice by publication in the LONDON GAZETTE (q.v.)

gazumping

The act of withdrawing from the sale of a house which has been agreed in principle, but before the last formalities have been carried out, so that the owner can sell elsewhere for a higher price.

general agent
> A representative who has a general authority to act within certain limits.

General Agreement on Tariffs and Trade (G.A.T.T.)
> An international treaty including the majority of world trading nations working together with the general aim of reducing tariff barriers and overcoming trading problems.

General Assembly
> One of the principal organs of the UNITED NATIONS (q.v.), in effect the forum for the representatives of all member states.

general average
> The sharing of a loss equally between all persons having a pecuniary interest in the preservation of a ship and its cargo, where the loss was the result of a voluntary sacrifice made for the benefit of all parties.

general crossing
> A crossing on a cheque having two parallel lines, with or without the phrases 'and company', 'not negotiable' or 'account payee only'. Such a cheque is only payable to the credit of a bank account.

general eyre
> In medieval times, a periodical enquiry made in each locality by travelling officials into matters of an administrative and legal nature.

General Court Martial
> A court exercising military law in cases of a more serious nature.

general damages
> The sum of money actually required to compensate an injured person for loss or damage.

general legacy
> The gift by will of something not specifically identified, for example 'one of my motor cars', or '£1000'.

general lien

The lawful retention of goods until all debts due from the owner to the possessor have been paid. An example would be a solicitor's lien over a client's papers until his fees have been paid.

general meeting

A meeting of all members of a company. The term includes both Statutory Meetings, Annual General Meetings, and EXTRA-ORDINARY MEETINGS (q.v.)

general partner

A member of a PARTNERSHIP (q.v.), who takes part fully in its activities.

General Register Office

The official body appointed by the State for the maintenance of important statistical information.

General Synod

A body of the established Church of England which has replaced the Church Assembly. It enjoys the right to pass measures having the force of law.

general warrant

A warrant not naming the person to be arrested, traditionally illegal in this country.

genocide

Acts taken in furtherance of a policy of wiping out a particular race, which are illegal under international law.

gentleman's agreement

Sometimes used in situations where the parties do not intend to create legally binding relationships.

gift inter vivos

A gift made during the lifetime of the donor.

gilt-edged market

Dealings in first-class securities such as Government stocks or municipal authorities' stocks, which are backed by the Government.

gilt-edged securities
>   Securities of the United Kingdom government or of important local and municipal authorities.

giro
>   A simplified form of money transfer through banks and post-offices.

Glasgow beer duty
>   A temporary exise duty of 2 Scots pence (or 1/6 of an English penny) imposed in 1693 on beer sold within the town of Glasgow, to raise money for the building of a quay from the Broomielaw to Duckel's Green.

going special
>   Said of a barrister appearing on a circuit or at sessions of which he is not a member. At one time this necessitated the payment of a special fee.

golden rule
>   A rule of interpretation for judges to apply to Acts of Parliament, whereby they are to be interpreted according to their ordinary, plain meaning, unless this would lead to absurdity.

gold standard
>   The principle that a nation's paper currency has a definite value in gold. It was abandoned by the United Kingdom in 1931.

good faith
>   Generally used in the sense of honesty, as applied to some course of conduct or action.

goods on consignment
>   Goods sent from one country to an agent in another country, for sale by the agent, who remits nett proceeds to his supplier.

goodwill
>   The advantages accruing to a business from its reputation and connections.

Government Chemist

A public official who takes samples and makes analyses on behalf of government departments.

Government Legal Service

An arm of the Civil Service open to both barristers and solicitors. Its members are attached to various Government Departments to provide legal services such as advice and advocacy.

governor-general

The person appointed in an independent Commonwealth country to exercise the functions of head of state on behalf of the Queen.

grain cargo

A cargo of which the portion consisting of grain is more than ⅓ of the registered tonnage of the ship.

grand assize

A medieval procedure by which twelve knights were elected to decide in a dispute over land ownership whether or not the contents of a writ were true.

grand jury

A panel of 12 knights in each locality who in the Middle Ages presented details of crimes of which they had some knowledge.

grant caeterorum

A grant of probate to executors, other than to an executor appointed to deal only with certain assets by way of limited probate.

grant durante dementia

A temporary grant of probate made during the insanity of an executor.

grant durante minore aetate

A temporary grant of probate made while an executor is under the age of majority.

grant of probate

The process of formal proof of a will for which an executor

must apply on the death of the maker of the will. The grant is issued by a Registrar.

grant save and except

A grant of probate made to an executor appointed to deal only with particular assets, and omitting the part of the estate appointed for the other executors.

grantee

In respect of a BILL OF SALE (q.v.), the person is whose favour the bill of sale is granted.

grantor

In respect of a bill of sale, the person assigning an interest in personal property.

grape must

Unfermented grape juice.

gratuitous promise

A promise not enforceable under English law due to a lack of CONSIDERATION (q.v.)

Gray's Inn

One of the four societies entitled to admit people to the rank of barrister by calling them to the Bar. Traditionally the Inn for provincial practitioners.

Great Britain

Scotland, England and Wales, united in 1707 as the Kingdom of Great Britain.

Great Seal

The device by which the Chancellor in medieval times endorsed writs in the King's name.

Green Book

The publication containing the procedural rules of the County Court.

green form scheme

A limited system for legal advice and assistance, often used as a first step to obtaining full legal aid for a particular case.

Green Paper

A Command Paper containing proposals for future governmental policy, as a basis for discussion.

green pound

An expression used within the Common Market for the rate of exchange at which prices agreed for the COMMON AGRICULTURAL POLICY (q.v.) are converted into pounds.

grievous bodily harm (G.B.H.)

The crime of causing serious physical harm to another person.

gross domestic product

The total amount of goods and services which a state produces during a particular period.

gross national product

The total amount of goods and services produced in a particular state over a given period, plus or minus the balance on external trade.

gross profit

The total of any profits before expenses are deducted.

group accounts

A statement which must be prepared and laid before a general meeting each year by a company controlling SUBSIDIARIES (q.v.) other than WHOLLY OWNED SUBSIDIARIES (q.v.)

guarantee

A promise to pay any loss arising from a transaction, where the person making the promise is not connected with the transaction.

guarantee company

A company the liability of whose members is limited by the amount each has undertaken to contribute in the event of a winding-up.

guarantor

A person undertaking to be responsible for the debt or default of someone else.

guardian ad litem

A responsible person appointed to protect the interests of a defendant in a civil case, such as a child, who is unable to deal with the matter on his own account.

guillotine

A resolution of the House of Commons closing the debate on a Bill after a certain period of time.

guilty

The verdict in a criminal case which means that the offence alleged is found to be true, and the person accused is as a result convicted.

guilty but insane

A verdict at one time available in criminal cases, whereby the accused was found not to be capable of forming the necessary criminal intent. It amounted to an aquittal, but there could be no appeal against it.

H

habendum *(Lat.)*

A clause in a conveyance specifying the estate which is to be assigned to a purchaser.

habeas corpus *(Lat.)*

A PREROGATIVE WRIT (q.v.) to obtain the release of someone who has been unlawfully detained in prison or elsewhere.

hammering

The act of suspending a member of the Stock Exchange who has defaulted or been found guilty of unbecoming conduct.

handling stolen goods

The criminal offence of knowingly receiving goods which have been stolen, or making arrangements for their disposal.

Hansard

The official report of proceedings in the House of Lords and the House of Commons.

harbour authority

Collectively, the officials charged with the maintenance and management of a harbour.

head licence

The first licence granted by an owner of a patent, copyright or similar rights, to someone making use of them. That user may himself grant sub-licences.

headnote

The summary appearing at the commencement of a law report indicating what the case is about by abbreviating the facts and decision.

heads of agreement

The main points of a commercial agreement noted as a preliminary step, which are to be drawn up more fully at a later date.

hearsay evidence

The testimony of a witness whose evidence has not been obtained from personal experience but completely from another person or persons.

hearing in camera

A court hearing in private, usually ordered only in legitimacy and nullity matters, and in cases dealing with children.

hearth tax

An assessed tax of two shillings a year imposed in 1662 on every hearth and stove in dwelling houses in England and Wales. It was repealed in 1689.

hedging

A dealer's technique of attempting to ensure a normal trading profit, by covering himself against any speculative fluctuations due to price changes.

Her Majesty in Council

The JUDICIAL COMMITTEE OF THE PRIVY COUNCIL (q.v.).

he who comes to equity must come with clean hands

The principle that a person who seeks assistance by application of the rules of EQUITY (q.v.), must himself not have acted improperly.

he who seeks equity must do equity

The principle that a person who seeks assistance by application of the rules of EQUITY (q.v.), must himself be seen to act properly.

High Court
>The senior level of trial in civil matters, comprising the Queen's Bench, Chancery and Family Divisions.

High Court of Justiciary
>The supreme court of criminal jurisdiction in Scotland.

highjacking
>The unlawful taking over of control of an aircraft, which is a criminal act under the laws of England.

high seas
>The oceans of the world beyond the jurisdiction of any country's territorial waters.

High Sheriff
>The official responsible for putting in the bailiffs by execution of process, who also presides over the SHERIFF'S COURT (q.v.)

highway
>A right of way or passage open to all subjects of the sovereign.

hire-purchase
>An agreement to hire goods for a certain period by paying specified instalments, at the end of which the customer has the option to buy them.

holder
>In connection with a negotiable instrument such as a cheque or bill of exchange, the person in whose favour it is payable, or to whom it has been endorsed, and who also has possession of it.

holder in due course
>A person entitled to accept a negotiable instrument free from rights of third parties, by accepting it in good faith and without notice of any defect.

holding charge
>A criminal charge brought in respect of a lesser offence, while a more serious offence is under investigation.

holding company

A company which controls a SUBSIDIARY COMPANY (q.v.), either through its board, or by holding more than fifty per cent of its share capital.

holding out

The act of suggesting that a particular situation exists, in the hope that another person will rely on it.

Home Circuit

The South-Eastern Circuit of the Bar, and one of the six Circuits to which a barrister may belong.

home trade ship

A ship engaged in trading between the United Kingdom, and the coast of mainland Europe between the River Elbe and Brest.

homicide

A killing, either lawful or unlawful.

honour policy

A type of marine insurance with a gambling element, where the assured has no insurable interest. Strictly speaking illegal and certainly unenforceable, but still issued and honoured.

horizontal integration

The linking-up of organisations following the same line of business, so as to cut back on costs.

hospital ship

A vessel for carrying the sick, wounded or shipwrecked, exempt from capture in international law.

hotchpot

The process of taking into account a sum previously advanced to a beneficiary under a will by the maker of it, so as to create fairness among all entitled to benefit under the will.

hot pursuit

In international law, the right of pursuing a ship which has committed an offence in TERRITORIAL WATERS (q.v.), and following it onto the HIGH SEAS (q.v.)

household effects
Furniture and other articles of ordinary and domestic use, including PERSONAL EFFECTS (q.v.), moved with someone who is transferring residence to this country.

House of Commons Offices Commission
A committee which controls the working conditions of the permanent staff of the House of Commons.

House of Lords
(1) The highest court in the country in both civil and criminal cases.
(2) The upper house of the two Houses of Parliament.

House of Lords Offices Committee
A body which controls the conditions of service of the permanent staff of the House of Lords, and the accommodation which it uses.

hundred
The ancient division of each county into smaller units, called 'hundreds', for the purposes of administration.

hundred court
Ancient court of limited powers with jurisdiction only within a particular hundred, or division of a county.

Hungary water
A spirit compounded with flowers of rosemary.

hung jury
Popular expression for a jury which is unable to arrive at a firm decision.

husband and wife
An expression for the branch of law governing matrimonial proceedings between the parties to a marriage.

hybrid bill
A PUBLIC BILL (q.v.) receiving Parliamentary consideration which also concerns private interests.

hybrid offence
>A criminal offence which can be tried either by magistrates or by a jury.

hydrocarbon oils
>Materials such as petrol products, coal tar and oils produced from coal, shale, peat, other bituminous substances and all liquid hydrocarbons. Examples are petrol and diesel oil. They constitute an important part of the revenue of central government.

hydrometer
>An instrument used to determine the strength and specific gravity of wines and spirits.

hypothecation
>The giving of something as a pledge or security for a debt, but without giving up possession of it.

I

ibid. *(Lat.)*

In the same place as that previously mentioned.

idem *(Lat.)*

The identical person or thing.

ignorantia juris neminem excusat *(Lat.)*

Ignorance of the law is no excuse.

illegal contract

An agreement totally without effect in law, for example an agreement to commit a crime or to break a rule of law.

illegitimacy

In general, the state of being unlawful or illegal; in particular, applied to children born out of wedlock, who prior to 1969 were in a less favourable position to succeed to intestate property than legitimate children.

immature spirits

Spirits which have not been kept in warehouse for a period of at least three years.

immemorial existence

The fictional beginning of legal memory, fixed as being in 1189, at the start of the reign of King Richard I.

immigration officer

An official employed by the Home Office to control the arrival of aliens at sea and airports in the United Kingdom.

immoveable property
Land and leasehold interests, as opposed to objects and goods.

impeachment
A former criminal proceeding brought against peers of the realm in the House of Lords for treason or felony.

imperfect entry
A provisional customs entry by which an importer can land and examine goods under surveillance, where he has not sufficient information about them to make a full customs declaration. Also known as a bill of sight.

imperial preference
The former system whereby goods originating in the Commonwealth were admitted duty-free or at favourable rates of duty into the United Kingdom.

implied malice
In relation to murder, the intention to inflict grievous bodily harm.

implied trust
A trust arising where one person buys property, and has it transferred into the name of another person.

importation
The act of bringing into this country something from any territory abroad.

import duty
An *ad valorem* tax imposed on goods imported into the United Kingdom, assessed as a percentage of their value.

import licence
A permit to import a particular article, the bringing of which into the country would otherwise be prohibited or restricted.

importuning
Canvassing for someone to commit a sexual act, generally of an illicit nature.

impost
>   Formerly a term for an additional duty of customs.

in bonis *(Lat.)*
>   In connection with the goods or estate of someone who has died.

incest
>   Sexual intercourse between people within the prohibited degrees of relationship. Thus a man may not have sexual intercourse with his mother, sister, daughter or grandmother.

Inchmaree clause
>   A clause in a policy of marine insurance making underwriters liable for loss caused by certain prescribed matters in addition to those in the standard form of policy.

inchoate instrument
>   A negotiable instrument such as a bill of exchange which is incomplete in some way.

inchoate offence
>   A crime which has not necessarily been carried through to completion, such as a conspiracy or an attempt.

inch of candle
>   Formerly a means of valuing goods imported by the East India Company. They were offered for sale in the City of London, and sold at the highest offer made during the burning of an inch of candle.

incitement
>   The encouragement of another person to carry out an illegal activity, which is itself a criminal offence.

incitement to disaffection
>   A criminal offence constituted by the attempt to dissuade a member of the armed forces from his duty or allegiance, or by possessing documents which might have that effect if distributed among members of the armed forces.

income and expenditure account
A statement which every company not trading for profit must put before its members in general meeting every year, giving a true picture of its income and expenditure.

income tax
A tax levied directly on income and earnings, and administered by the Inland Revenue. First imposed in 1799.

in consimili casu *(Lat.)*
In a similar case.

inconvertible banknotes
Notes without the legal right to exchange them for their face value in gold, for example modern banknotes of the United Kingdom.

Incorporated Council of Law Reporting
The body controlling the preparation and production of the official law reports.

incorporation
The registration of a company with limited liability.

incorporeal chattels
Rights in or over things such as company shares, which are intangible, and can only be enforced by legal action.

incorrigible rogue
An ancient device for committing persistent wrongdoers to custody (by putting them into this category).

incumbrance
Some liability affecting goods or property, such as a mortgage.

in custodia legis *(Lat.)*
In legal custody.

indebitatus assumpsit *(Lat.)*
An ancient action to recover a particular sum of money.

indecent assault

The crime of committing an assault on a female, together with an act of indecency.

indecent exposure

The displaying of sexual organs by a man or woman, with the intention or effect of insulting a member of the opposite sex.

in delicto *(Lat.)*

At fault.

indemnity

A promise to pay any loss arising from a transaction, where the person making the promise is connected with that transaction.

indent

Instructions regarding particulars of goods to be purchased, and the price which is to be paid.

indentures

An agreement drawing up the terms of an apprenticeship between the person apprenticed and his master.

independent contractor

One who performs a given task on his own account and under his own control, as opposed to an employee, who must work as his employer directs.

index vectigalium *(Lat.)*

A summary of duties published in 1670 by the farmers of the customs.

indicia *(Lat.)*

Signs; indications.

indictment

A formal statement of a serious crime prepared for a trial by jury.

indictable offence

A serious criminal offence which can be tried only by a Crown Court.

indorsement

(1) Generally, a signature; particularly, it refers to the transfer of entitlement under a cheque or BILL OF EXCHANGE (q.v.)

(2) In relation to traffic offences, the noting on a driving licence of the details of an offence which the driver has committed. (q.v. ENDORSEMENT.)

indorsement of a writ

A statement on a writ of summons making clear the claim that is being made in a civil case, and the relief which is being asked for.

indorser

The person who makes an indorsement.

industrial death benefit

A state benefit payable to dependants of employees who die because of an accident at work or some industrial disease.

industrial disablement benefit

A state benefit payable to employees who are disabled due to some accident at work, or some industrial disease due to their work.

industrial injury benefit

A state benefit payable to employees who are unable to work because of accidents at work or some industrial diseases due to their work.

industrial injury compensation

Money paid by an employer to people injured while working for him, because he did not fulfil his legal duties.

industrial property

A generic name for property rights such as patents, trade marks and registered designs. Sometimes it is also extended to include copyright.

industrial tribunal

A body which adjudicates on complaints by employees that they have been unfairly dismissed by their employers.

in esse *(Lat.)*

In being; in existence.

inevitable accident

A collision at sea brought about by an ACT OF GOD (q.v.)

in extenso *(Lat.)*

Fully; at length.

infant

The former term for a minor, or person under the age of eighteen.

infanticide

A criminal offence committed by a woman who causes the death of her child while it is under the age of twelve months, and who has not recovered from the effect of childbirth.

inferior court of record

A lower court such as a county court which is the subject of supervision by a higher court.

in flagrante delicto *(Lat.)*

The condition of being caught in the act of doing something, usually of a criminal or reprehensible nature.

information

The stage prior to the issue of a summons by a magistrate by which a statement or information of the offence complained of is put before a justice of the peace by the individual who is making the complaint, or by the prosecutor.

infra *(Lat.)*

Below; underneath.

infringement

The act of using without authorisation another person's monopoly right, such as a copyright work or a patented invention.

in futuro *(Lat.)*

At some time in the future.

ingrosser
>A person who bought commodities in order to sell them at a later date.

inhabited house duty
>An assessed tax first imposed in 1696, at varying rates. It continued in differing forms until finally abolished in 1924.

injunction
>An order restraining a person from doing a particular act.

injuria sine damno *(Lat.)*
>A breach of a legal right which does not result in injury or damage.

injurious falsehood
>A civil action in respect of a false statement made intentionally, which has caused loss to the person deceived.

inland bill
>A BILL OF EXCHANGE (q.v.) which is both drawn and payable inside the United Kingdom.

inland navigation
>Navigation which is not within the limits of a customs port.

Inland Revenue
>The Department of State responsible for the administration of direct taxes such as income tax.

in limine *(Lat.)*
>At the edge; at the beginning.

in loco parentis *(Lat.)*
>The condition of acting in place of a parent towards a particular child.

in minore delicto *(Lat.)*
>Applied to a person who is less to blame than someone else.

Inner Temple
>One of the four societies entitled to admit people to the rank of barrister by calling them to the Bar.

innocent misrepresentation
A false statement honestly believed in at the time it was made.

innovation
The continuing development of the process of invention under the umbrella of the patent system.

Inns of Court
The four societies entitled to admit people to the rank of barrister by calling them to the Bar, namely Grays Inn, Lincolns Inn, the Middle Temple and the Inner Temple.

innuendo
Words which are not in their normal meaning defamatory, but which may transmit a defamatory meaning to the person at whom they are directed.

in pari delicto *(Lat.)*
Of equal blame.

in pari materia *(Lat.)*
In the same situation.

in personam *(Lat.)*
In respect of a person, where some legal action is concerned.

in pleno *(Lat.)*
Completely; in full.

in praesenti *(Lat.)*
Currently; now; at the present time.

in propria persona *(Lat.)*
In one's own capacity.

input tax
The VALUE ADDED TAX (q.v.) paid by the person receiving a supply of goods or services to the person making the supply.

inquest
An enquiry conducted by a coroner and his jury into cases of sudden death and TREASURE TROVE (q.v.)

in re *(Lat.)*
> Concerning; in the case of.

in rem *(Lat.)*
> In respect of an object or thing, where some legal action is concerned.

inscribed security
> Stocks or shares the title to which is evidenced by a book entry.

inscrutable accident
> A collision at sea brought about by unknown causes, or in such circumstances that it is impossible to apportion the blame.

insolvency
> The state of being unable to pay one's debts.

in specie *(Lat.)*
> In its own form; in coin.

inspection
> The viewing of a particular site or objects by a judge or jury or both, which may be ordered during the course of a trial.

Inspector of Taxes
> A full-time civil servant appointed by the Board of Inland Revenue, responsible for the issue of assessments of income tax.

inspector's bail
> The release of a person arrested without warrant on a less serious charge by the officer in charge of a police station, where the person arrested will not be brought before a court within 24 hours.

in statu quo ante *(Lat.)*
> In the condition in which something was in before a certain point in time or event.

Institute of Legal Executives
> An organisation to promote the interests of non-professionnal employees in the offices of solicitors; it operates its own system of examinations for membership either as Associate or Fellow.

institutional investor

An organisation such as a pension fund or insurance company which regularly draws in large sums of money to invest in securities.

instructions

The case presented by a solicitor to a barrister whom he has retained or instructed to act for his lay client. Instructions are also given by a lay client to his solicitor.

insurable interest

The principle that a person seeking protection under a contract of insurance must have a financial interest in the event against which he wishes to obtain cover.

insurance

The undertaking by one person (the insurer) to pay money or confer a benefit on another person (the insured) on the happening of a certain event. Usually applied to contracts of indemnity where an event such as a fire may or may not take place.

insured

A person who stands to receive a sum of money or other benefit from another person (the insurer, assurer or underwriter) on the happening of a certain event.

insurer

One who undertakes to pay a sum of money or confer a benefit on another person (the insured) on the happening of a certain event.

intangible assets

Property appearing in the accounts of a business which is incapable of physical existence. Examples are copyright and goodwill.

intellectual property

A generic expression for property rights such as copyright, registered designs, trade marks and patents.

inter alia *(Lat.)*

Among other things.

inter alios *(Lat.)*
>   Among other people.

interest
>   Money paid, generally at a fixed rate, in return for the loan of a sum of money.

interest reipublicae ut sit finis litium *(Lat.)*
>   It is in the common interest that law suits should reach a final conclusion. (Literally 'that there should be an end to litigation'.)

interference with contractual relations
>   A cause of action against a person who maliciously and without lawful justification persuades another person to commit a breach of contract, and thus damage the other party.

interim dividend
>   The distribution of profits in hand during the course of a company's financial year, where the directors are confident that a dividend will be declared at the end of the year.

interlocutory injunction
>   A court order which takes effect only until the trial of the main action.

interlocutory matter
>   An interim or secondary dispute or issue arising during the course of proceedings.

international coasting voyage
>   A journey between two countries in the course of which the vessel does not go more than 20 miles from land.

International Court of Justice
>   An organ of the United Nations responsible for settling disputes between member states.

international flight
>   A flight from an airport in the United Kingdom to an airport situated abroad (or vice-versa).

International Labour Organisation
An organisation of the United Nations dedicated to the improvement of working conditions in every country.

International Monetary Fund (I.M.F.)
An international organisation aiming to increase international trade and achieve solidarity between national currencies.

international voyage
A voyage from a seaport in the United Kingdom to a seaport in a foreign country (or vice-versa).

inter partes *(Lat.)*
Between the parties.

interpleader proceedings
A court hearing to decide conflicting claims over goods seized in EXECUTION (q.v.) of a court order, or goods already the subject of court proceedings.

inter praesentes *(Lat.)*
Between those people present.

interrogatories
Lists of formal questions delivered by one side to a civil dispute which the other side is obliged to answer.

inter se *(Lat.)*
'Between themselves', generally with reference to a relationship between certain people.

in terrorem *(Lat.)*
By means of threat; intended as a threat.

intervention price
An expression used within the Common Market to indicate the price level at which support buying for any commodity can take place for the purposes of the Common Agricultural Policy.

inter vivos *(Lat.)*
Among the living, generally said in respect of a gift in settlement.

intestacy
>   The condition of having died without having made a will.

intestate succession
>   The transfer of a person's property on death according to fixed legal rules, where that person has made no will.

intimidation
>   The infliction of harm by illegal threats which interfere with the lawful freedom of others to do as they please.

in toto *(Lat.)*
>   Wholly; completely.

intoxicating liquor
>   Alcoholic drink, which cannot legally be sold without an excise licence.

intoxication
>   A factor to be considered in criminal cases in deciding whether the person accused is capable of forming the necessary criminal intention.

in transitu *(Lat.)*
>   Of goods, in the course of being delivered from seller to buyer.

intra vires *(Lat.)*
>   Within the scope of prescribed powers (generally in relation to an act).

inutility
>   A ground for rejecting an application for a patent, on the basis that it serves no useful purpose.

in vacuo *(Lat.)*
>   An abstract reference, without application to the particular circumstances.

invalid care allowance
>   A state benefit payable to men and single women of working age who have had to stay home without employment to care for a severely disabled person.

invalidity benefit

A state benefit payable to people who have been receiving sickness benefit for more than 6 months.

invasion of privacy

Often suggested as a possible new civil right of action, but not yet established in England and Wales. An example, if introduced, might be the right not to be photographed against one's will.

invert sugar

Cane sugar changed from a non-fermentable to a fermentable form.

investment trust

A company inviting subscriptions for its shares, and placing sums received in a wide range of investments.

invisible trade

The export and import of services (as opposed to goods).

invitee

A person who has accepted an invitation, generally to enter the premises of another person.

involuntary manslaughter

A category of cases where death was caused in circumstances which the person responsible foresaw might cause physical but not fatal harm, and which had no lawful excuse.

inward clearing bill

A certificate given to a ship's master acknowledging that all customs requirements have been complied with by a ship arriving from abroad.

inward processing

The importation of goods into the United Kingdom in one form, so that work can be carried out, after which they are exported in another form.

I.O.U.

A simple acknowledgement of a debt, which is neither a receipt, a negotiable instrument nor an agreement.

ipso facto *(Lat.)*
> By the very fact itself.

irretrievable breakdown of marriage
> The only ground now existing for divorce, but evidenced by matters such as desertion, cruelty and adultery.

issue
> (1) A person's offspring, now including illegitimate children.
> (2) The point which is the subject of an argument.

issued capital
> The nominal value of shares which are actually issued in a limited company.

issuing house
> An institution such as a merchant bank arranging public issues of new shares and stocks.

itinerant justices
> The judicial representatives of the King, who in the Middle Ages travelled about the country trying cases in various centres.

J

jactitation of marriage

An unjustified boast made by someone that he or she is married to a particular person. At one time it gave rise to a cause of action.

Janson clause

A clause in a policy of marine insurance making a stated percentage of loss deductible from all claims for PARTICULAR AVERAGE (q.v.), the UNDERWRITERS (q.v.) being liable only for the excess.

jetsam

Cargo thrown overboard from a vessel and which remains on the surface of the water.

jettison

The throwing of goods overboard, in order to save a vessel or the remainder of its cargo.

jobber

A member of the Stock Exchange who does business with other jobbers and with stockbrokers relating solely to the sale and purchase of stock. He does not deal directly with the public.

jobber's turn

The difference between the price at which a JOBBER (q.v.) is prepared to buy stock, and that at which he is prepared to sell it.

job release
>A state benefit payable to men and women of certain ages, who leave work before state pension age, and who are replaced by persons registered as unemployed.

joinder of actions
>The linking up of separately commenced court cases on the ground that they are sufficiently close in subject-matter and circumstances.

joint and several liability
>A situation in which a person having a claim against a number of people can sue them all together, or proceed separately against each.

Joint Committee on Consolidation Bills
>A joint committee of both Houses of Parliament which examines all CONSOLIDATING BILLS (q.v.) and similar measures put forward in each session.

joint legal profession
>The system existing in the great majority of countries outside Britain, where there is a single united legal profession.

joint lives policy
>A policy of life assurance on the lives of two or more people, which is payable on the death of the first person.

joint stock company
>A company trading with a permanent joint stock, subscribed by members in the form of transferable shares of fixed amounts.

joint tenancy
>Where the share of one of several owners passes on his death to the surviving owners.

joint tortfeasors
>Persons whose shares in the commission of a civil wrong are in furtherance of a common intention.

joint will
>A will, made by two or more people.

Journal Office

A group of clerks in the House of Commons which undertakes research and produces the JOURNALS (q.v.)

Journals

The official record of proceedings of the House of Commons. An equivalent record of proceedings is kept for proceedings in the House of Lords.

Judge-Advocate General

A lawyer appointed to control all matters relating to military justice in the Army and the Royal Air Force.

Judge-Advocate of the Fleet

The lawyer appointed to control all matters of administration of naval law.

judge in chambers

A judge not sitting in open court, but for the private hearing of special business.

judge-made law

Decisions in cases which become precedents, and part of the law of the country; this is a particular feature of the English legal system.

judgement creditor

Someone who has obtained a court order for the payment of a sum of money.

judgement debtor

One who owes money as a result of a court's decision against him.

judgement in default

A formal decision in favour of a person who has made a claim, where the other side has not defended it.

judgement summons

A court action against a JUDGEMENT DEBTOR (q.v.) in respect of the money owed.

Judicial Committee of the Privy Council
> Formerly the final appeal court for most Dominions; but now only for appeals from certain British dependencies and colonies.

judicial immunity
> The exemption granted to judges from all liability for acts done in the execution of their judicial functions.

judicial notice
> The principle that a judge will take for granted matters of such common knowledge that no strict proof of them is necessary.

judicial precedent
> The system whereby the judgement of a court is binding on lower courts until overruled by a higher court or by Parliament.

judicial review
> An application to the High Court seeking to correct an alleged defect in procedure of a lower court, tribunal or public body.

judicial separation
> A court order that a husband and wife should no longer live together; it does not however amount to a formal divorce.

judiciary
> The judges who interpret and administer the law. As a body they form one of the three powers of government.

junior
> Any barrister other than a Queen's Counsel, who may in fact be of considerable seniority and experience.

jurat *(Lat.)*
> A short statement on an AFFIDAVIT (q.v.) recording by whom it was sworn, before whom, and the date and place of swearing.

jurisprudence
> The methodical study of the phrases and expressions used by lawyers.

juristic person

A legal person other than a human being, for example a corporation.

juror

A member of a jury; a juryman.

jury

A fixed number of people summoned to sit in court and give a decision on matters of fact.

jury of matrons

A jury of women formerly sworn to decide whether a female who had been condemned to death was pregnant, and thus able to escape hanging.

jus *(Lat.)*

A legal right.

jus accrescendi *(Lat.)*

In respect of tenants in common, the right of accrual where one survivor takes the whole property, on the death of the other.

jus gentium *(Lat.)*

The law of nations; the law of mankind.

jus in personam *(Lat.)*

A right enforceable against a particular person.

jus in rem *(Lat.)*

A right in respect of property, as opposed to a right against a person.

jus tertii *(Lat.)*

A right enjoyed by a third person.

justice in Eyre

A judicial officer in medieval times with jurisdiction both in judicial matters and questions of local government.

justice itinerant

A medieval judge who travelled the kingdom administering the law of the monarch.

justice of the peace
> An unpaid magistrate appointed by the Lord Chancellor, on the recommendation of local advisory committees. Otherwise known as a J.P.

justifiable homicide
> The carrying out of a lawful sentence of death on a convicted criminal; also certain acts taken in defence of person or property.

justification
> A defence to an action for DEFAMATION (q.v.) whereby the words complained of are shown by the defence to be true.

juvenile court
> A court of magistrates or justices of the peace sitting under special conditions to hear a case against a person under 17.

juvenile court panel
> A group of magistrates (justices of the peace) existing in each Magistrates Court Division to deal with cases against persons under 17.

K

Kaffirs

Shares in companies operating in South Africa, particularly in the mining sector.

kangaroo

A procedure in Parliamentary committees by which a selection of amendments are considered for discussion, and the rest passed over.

kangaroo court

A popular expression for a rigged trial, generally of an unofficial nature. An example would be a group of employees purporting to try one of their workmates.

keeping a disorderly house

The criminal offence of operating a brothel.

keeping house

Applied to the case of an insolvent debtor who adopts the practice of shutting himself indoors, and not answering to callers.

Kennedy Round

A stage in tariff reduction and removal of trade barriers, which formed part of the development of the GENERAL AGREEMENT ON TARIFFS AND TRADE (q.v.)

King's Inn, Dublin
> The body which calls barristers of the Republic of Ireland to the Bar.

King's Peace
> In medieval times, the jurisdiction which the king enjoyed to bring any disputes into his own courts for trial.

kleptomania
> The irresistible urge to steal, which can amount to a form of insanity.

knock-for-knock agreement
> An agreement between two or more insurance companies that each will bear the loss of people insured with it, rather than take legal action against the other insurance company.

know-how
> Technical skill, experience or production details which may become the subject of a licensing agreement.

L

laches

Unreasonable delay in taking advantage of a legal remedy which prevents the person entitled to it from taking action at a later time.

laesio fidei *(Lat.)*

A breaking of trust or faith.

land certificate

A document setting out the quality of a person's title to land, the property involved, and any registered charge.

land charge

Something affecting proprietary rights in land, such as a restrictive covenant or an option to purchase.

landing charges

The initial charges incurred for the off-loading of imported goods.

landlord and tenant

A popular expression for disputes relating to property rights in respect of lettings, concerning particularly the fixing of rent and obtaining of possession.

Land Registry

A system of local offices investigating, controlling and recording matters relating to registered land.

landside
> The area of an airport open to the general public before out-going passengers pass through customs control.

lapsed legacy
> A gift in a will to a person who dies before the maker of the will.

lapsed policy
> An insurance policy which has been discontinued because payments have not been kept up.

larceny
> A former crime involving the taking and carrying away of goods without the consent of the owner, now replaced by the law of theft.

last survivor and survivorship policy
> A policy of life assurance on the lives of two or more people, which is payable on the death of the last of them.

launching clause
> A provision in a policy of insurance specifying the risks accepted during the launching of a vessel.

law
> A body of rules of conduct which the state will enforce.

Law Commission
> The Law Commission Act 1965 introduced one Commission in London and another in Edinburgh, to keep the law under constant review, and to make recommendations for reform.

Law French
> A form of Anglo-Norman French which was the official language of the courts for some centuries after the Norman Conquest.

Law Journal Reports
> A now defunct series of law reports.

Law Latin
> Latin phrases having a technical meaning to lawyers, and which cannot always be translated accurately into English.

law merchant

The forerunner of mercantile or commercial law, originally based on the customs of merchants which were recognised in most countries.

Law Officers

Collectively, the political appointments of Attorney-General and the Solicitor-General. In Scotland, the Lord Advocate and the Solicitor-General for Scotland.

law of marque

The provisions of international law governing enemy property seized on the high seas.

law of the flag

The principle of treating a vessel according to the law of the nation under whose flag she sails.

law reform

The continuing process of improving the law to reflect contemporary needs, and of removing injustices or archaic rules.

Law Reform Committee

A permanent committee of judges and lawyers appointed to consider areas of law referred to it by the Lord Chancellor, or to consider questions of possible reform which they consider suitable.

Law Reports, the

In particular, a familiar term for the monthly reports published by the Incorporated Council of Law Reporting; in general, the collected case-law of the English legal system.

Law Society

The body governing the solicitors' profession.

Laws of Oleron

An ancient system of laws to control maritime matters which influenced a number of European systems, including that of England.

Law Times Reports

A defunct series of law reports. Nevertheless they contain older cases which are still of importance.

lay assessor

A layman with special expertise in particular fields brought in to assist legal chairmen in certain courts and tribunals hearing cases of a technical nature.

lay client

Used among barristers and judges to distinguish between a solicitor client and a member of the public who is the client of that solicitor.

laytime

The period during which a ship is loading or discharging in harbour.

leader

The more senior of a team of barristers conducting the case for one of the sides in a dispute. Often, but not necessarily, a Queen's Counsel.

Leader of the House

A position held by a senior member of the House of Commons, whose duties include overseeing the Government's legislative arrangements, and the matters to be considered each week by the House.

leading question

A question put by an advocate to his own witness which suggests the desired answer, and is therefore not acceptable under the rules of evidence.

League of Nations

The forerunner of the UNITED NATIONS (q.v.) and the first world association of sovereign states. Founded after the First World War, it ended with the Second World War.

leasehold

A right to exclusive possession of land, usually for a fixed term of years, and less than absolute ownership.

leasehold enfranchisement
> The right of a long-term lessee at a low rent to obtain the freehold or a longer tenancy of the property which he occupies.

legacy
> The giving of personal property in goods under a will, as opposed to a gift of land.

Legal Aid
> The official state scheme allowing people below certain income and property levels to obtain assistance with legal costs.

legal estate in land
> For practical purposes, either a freehold or a leasehold interest.

legal executive
> A member of a solicitor's staff who is not himself an admitted solicitor or an articled clerk. Formerly known as a managing clerk.

legal mortgage
> The tendering of land as security for a loan, so that a legal interest in that land is established in favour of the lender.

legal mortgage of shares
> The transfer of shares to a lender as security for a loan, registering the shares in his name and giving him the legal title.

legal personality
> The state of being affected in law by rights and duties. Companies and associations as well as humans are affected.

legal tender
> Coins or Bank of England notes of current validity.

legal treatise
> An authoritative commentary on a branch of the law in a book form, which has influenced the development of legal thought in that area.

legal weight

The weight of goods and their immediate wrappings taken together.

legatee

The recipient of a legacy or gift of goods in a will.

legal writer

A lawyer whose research and commentaries on the law are published in the form of textbooks and articles, which may assist in the development of that branch of the law.

legislation

Written rules enacted by Parliament or a subordinate law-making body.

legislation clause

A provision in international chartering agreements allowing cancellation if discrimination against foreign shipping is introduced.

legislature

The body resposible for making and amending laws, which in the United Kingdom consists of the two Houses of Parliament.

legitimacy

(1) A form of proceedings which may be brought seeking a declaration that a particular person or one of his ancestors has become of legitimate birth.

(2) The condition of being of legitimate birth.

legitimation

The condition granted to a child originally born illegitimate of being made legitimate by the subsequent marriage of his parents.

letter before action

A final letter written by a person involved in a legal dispute, threatening action unless his request is complied with.

letter of credit

A procedure by which a buyer of goods in another country makes cash available in the exporting country, which the seller obtains by producing evidence of shipment to a bank.

letter of hypothecation

A document addressed to a bank setting out details of drafts relating to the shipment of goods.

letter of indication

A document of indentification used by a traveller holding a letter of credit, containing a specimen of his signature.

letters of administration

The grant of authority made to an administrator of an estate of someone who has died, where there is no will, or the will has not appointed an executor.

letters patent

Formal documents by which the Crown makes certain appointments, grants titles and gives patent rights to inventors.

letters of request

A formal document from the personal representative of a dead shareholder to the directors of a company, requesting the transfer of shares into his name without referring to his representative capacity.

levy execution

To seize goods in payment of a loan, acting under authority of the law.

levying war

An element of the criminal offence of TREASON (q.v.), widely construed to take in a range of activities which give aid or comfort to the Queen's enemies.

lex domicilii *(Lat.)*

The law applying in the territory in which a person is domiciled.

lex fori *(Lat.)*

The legal system applying in the particular court in which a case is being heard.

lex loci celebrationis *(Lat.)*

In matrimonial law, the legal system of the country in which the wedding was performed.

lex loci contractus *(Lat.)*
> The legal system applicable in the place where a particular contract was made.

lex loci delicti *(Lat.)*
> The legal system applying in the place where a particular wrong was carried out.

lex mercatoria *(Lat.)*
> The law merchant known in earlier centuries, based on the customs of merchants and traders, which were adopted by the courts as settled law.

lex non cogit ad impossibilia *(Lat.)*
> The law does not force a person to do the impossible.

lex scripta *(Lat.)*
> Written law, contained in Acts of Parliament as opposed to decided cases in the courts.

lex situs *(Lat.)*
> The legal system applying in the place where a particular thing is located.

liability clause
> The clause in a company's memorandum of association, which states that the liability of its members is limited, and which may not be altered.

libel
> A defamatory statement made in a written or permanent form, and including something which has been broadcast.

library of deposit
> One of the libraries entitled to a free copy of every new book published in the United Kingdom.

licence
> A contractual agreement by which a limited use rather than an outright sale is granted.

licence in land
> Permission to be on or to make some temporary use of land.

licensed lighterman

A lighterman authorised by the Commissioners of Customs and Excise to convey bonded goods from one dock to another.

licensing agreement

Often used as an alternative term for a licence, in the sense of the document by which some limited use of the subject-matter is granted, as opposed to an outright sale.

licensing justices

Magistrates exercising their powers to grant licences to premises for the sale of alcohol.

lien

The right of one person to possess or control property legally belonging to someone else. It usually arises in respect of money due.

lien on shares

The right of a company to sell shares not fully paid up, which belong to a shareholder who does not respond to a call on those shares.

life imprisonment

The sanction for murder since the abolition of the death penalty.

ligan (also ligin or lagan)

Property thrown overboard from a ship (jetsam) with a float attached, to enable it to be recovered in the future.

light dues

A charge levied on a ship to pay for the maintenance of navigational aids such as lighthouses and buoys.

limitation of actions

The principle that legal rights which one person has against someone else are extinguished after a certain period of time in which nothing is done to assert them.

limited company

A company with share capital, the liability of its members being confined to any amount unpaid on the shares they hold.

limited legal tender

A type of money which can be proffered to discharge debts up to a particular amount only.

limited liability

The principle by which the formation of a limited company protects its members from full personal liability.

limited partner

A member of a partnership who does not assume any management function, but whose liability is limited to his own investment.

limited probate

PROBATE (q.v.) granted only in respect of a particular purpose, for example, to deal with personal property alone.

limping marriage

A marriage which has come to an end in the eyes of one country's system of law, but which still exists in the view of another country's system of law. For example, one country may not recognise a particular ground for divorce, or the concept of divorce at all.

Lincoln's Inn

One of the four societies entitled to admit people to the rank of barrister by calling them to the Bar. It is traditionally the Inn for Chancery practitioners.

liqueur

A spirituous liquor which has been so altered in character by the addition of flavouring matter, that it can only be sold commercially under a promotional or commercial name.

liquidated damages

A pre-estimation of the damage likely to be sustained if there is any breach of an agreement.

liquidator

An official appointed by the Court on the winding-up of a company; if none is appointed, the OFFICIAL RECEIVER (q.v.) will act.

liquidator's cash book

 A record of ingoings and outgoings which a liquidator is obliged to maintain in a WINDING-UP (q.v.) of a company.

liquidator's record book

 An account of the administration of a winding-up which the liquidator is obliged to maintain.

liquidator's trading account

 A record of any business carried on by a company during winding-up proceedings, which must be maintained by the liquidator.

litera legis *(Lat.)*

 The express words of an Act of Parliament, which must be applied to the facts of a particular case.

litigant in person

 A party to a case, who can address a court on his own behalf without a barrister or solicitor.

litigation

 The process of taking a dispute for decision by the courts.

littoral rights

 The rights enjoyed by the owners of land bounding on tidal navigable waters.

Liverpool Cotton Exchange

 The chief market through which passed the cotton destined for the factories of Lancashire.

Liverpool Court of Passage

 A court formerly exercising jurisdiction in smaller cases in the Liverpool area.

Lloyd's List

 A daily newspaper of shipping interest published by Lloyd's underwriters.

Lloyd's List Law Reports

 A series of reports in decided cases in matters of specialist commercial interest.

Lloyd's S.G. policy
> The standard policy at Lloyd's for ships and goods.

loading broker
> A shipbroker acting at a port as representative for a shipowner to find and load cargoes for him.

loading time
> That period of time within which a vessel or vehicle is to be loaded.

load line
> A mark on the side of a ship indicating the maximum depth to which it is lawful to load it.

loan capital
> That part of the resources available to a business which does not consist of equity capital, preference shares or partners' capital.

lob
> A mixture of yeast and strong wort added to fermenting wash in order to increase the production of spirit.

Local Government Reports
> A series of law reports in cases which bear on matters relating particularly to the work of local authorities.

location
> In commercial law, a contract of hiring.

loc. cit. (loco citato) *(Lat.)*
> With reference to a passage in a book, 'in the place previously mentioned'.

lockage
> A charge made against a vessel as a kind of toll for passing through a particular lock.

locus in quo *(Lat.)*
> The place in which an event occured.

locus sigilli *(Lat.)*
> The position of the seal. (Used in connection with documents.)

locus standi *(Lat.)*
> The right to be heard and to make submissions on a matter in which the person making those submissions has a sufficient interest.

log book
> A document kept by the master of a registered British ship in order to record daily events relating to its passage.

loitering with intent
> Formerly a criminal offence under the old vagrancy legislation, but now abolished.

Lomé Convention
> An international agreement linking the states of the Common Market with third world countries with which there exist close ties. Many of these countries are ex-colonies.

London acceptance credit
> Credit facilities arranged at a London bank on behalf of a British exporter.

London diamond market
> The principal centre in the world for dealings in diamonds.

London foreign exchange market
> Dealers and brokers operating in the City of London for the exchange of currencies.

London Gazette
> The Government's official newspaper, for the publication of official news and announcements.

London Metal Exchange
> A market for dealing in non-precious metals, particularly tin, copper, lead and zinc.

London money market
> The banks, discount houses and merchant banks operating in the City of London to trade in credit and money.

London orphan duty
> A special levy on wine and coal shipped into London, for the benefit of orphans of the City of London. First levied in 1694, and abolished in 1889.

London rubber exchange
> A market for dealings between producers of rubber, and brokers and dealers in that commodity.

long-dated paper
> Applied to bills of exchange with a life of at least three months.

long room
> The room where public business is transacted in a Custom House.

Lord Advocate
> One of the two Law Officers of the Crown in Scotland, it being a political appointment.

Lord Chamberlain
> An official who prior to 1968 was responsible for the censorship of stage plays.

Lord Chancellor
> A member of the Government who presides over debates in the House of Lords and appoints judges. He has overall supervision of both divisions of the Court of Appeal, and of the Chancery Division of the High Court.

Lord Lieutenant
> The chief representative of the Queen within each county.

Lord Ordinary
> A judge sitting in the Outer House of the Court of Session in Scotland.

Lord Resident
> The chief judge of the Court of Session in Scotland.

Lords Spiritual
> The Archbishops of Canterbury and York, the Bishops of London, Durham and Winchester, and 21 other bishops of the Church of England who sit in the House of Lords.

Lords Temporal
> Members of the House of Lords other than the LORDS SPIRITUAL (q.v.)

loss adjuster
> A person who acts for an insurance company to discover the cause of a claim and establish the amount of damage.

loss leader
> Items in a shop priced below cost to lure customers into the habit of trading there.

lost or not lost
> A clause in a policy of marine insurance to cover the situation where a ship may be away from a port, and the parties to a contract are unaware if it is still in existence.

lottery
> A distribution of prizes by lot or chance.

low wines
> Spirits of the first extraction which are redistilled into drinkable spirits.

lump sum freight
> The full amount agreed between shipowner and charterer for the exclusive hire of a ship for a particular purpose.

lump sum provision
> A form of settlement of maintenance liabilities by providing a capital sum as an alternative or in addition to periodic payments.

Lutine bell
> The bell of the ship *Lutine*, which is formally rung on the floor of Lloyd's on the occasion of some grave or important announcement.

M

M1

The total of notes and coins in circulation in the United Kingdom, plus current bank accounts.

M3

The total of notes and coins in existence in the United Kingdom, plus current bank accounts and deposit accounts.

made wine

Any liquor made from fruit and sugar, and which has undergone a process of fermentation.

magistrate

A judicial officer who adjudicates in less serious criminal cases. There are both unpaid justices of the peace and stipendiary magistrates.

magistrates' clerk

An official, generally legally qualified, who administers a magistrate's court, and advises lay justices on the law.

magistrates' court

The venue for less serious criminal cases, also known as petty sessions. It has some civil jurisdiction.

maiden speech

The first speech made by a Member of Parliament on entering the House of Commons, during which, by tradition, he will not be interrupted.

maintenance

(1) Financial assistance given to a person involved in a legal action by someone not involved in it, no longer a criminal offence.

(2) Money paid by one partner in a former marriage for the support of the other partner, and/or any children.

maintenance pending suit

The amount of financial provision which must be made by a husband in matrimonial proceedings while the case is being prepared.

majority verdict

A decision of a jury by no less than ten to two, now acceptable and abolishing the traditional requirement of unanimity.

mala fide *(Lat.)*

In bad faith.

mala in se *(Lat.)*

Corrupt practices.

mala prohibita *(Lat.)*

Illegal practices.

malice

The intent to commit a criminal act or a civil wrong.

malice aforethought

Criminal intention, particularly in relation to murder.

malicious damage

The former criminal offence of damaging another person's property without lawful excuse, now replaced by CRIMINAL DAMAGE (q.v.)

malicious prosecution

A cause of action to compensate a person against whom criminal proceedings were maliciously instituted, without any reasonable cause.

malt

Grain steeped in water, allowed to germinate, and dried at a certain stage to stop germination.

malversion

Some form of misconduct by the holder of an official position.

managing clerk

A former term for an unadmitted assistant in a solicitor's office, now known as a legal executive.

managing director

Generally a full-time member of the board of a company, supervising the activities of the other directors.

mandamus *(Lat.)*

An order of the High Court to compel a body to carry out a duty imposed upon it.

mandate

A written authority under which someone gives another person authority to act for him.

mandated territory

A territory supervised by another country appointed at some time during its existence by the former League of Nations.

mandatory injunction

A court order to compel a certain act to be carried out.

manifest

A document containing full particulars of all items comprising the cargo of a ship or aircraft.

manorial courts

In medieval times, courts held by lords of the manor for the people who lived on their estates.

Manpower Services Commission

An official body whose function is to train men and women for employment.

manslaughter

The unlawful killing of a person without specific criminal intention.

mansuetae naturae *(Lat.)*

An expression applied to domestic animals, or those not of a dangerous species.

manufacturing clause

A provision of American law that most books in the English language by an American author have to be printed in the United States in order to obtain copyright protection there. It is now largely abolished.

manufacturing under licence

The procedure by which an inventor grants a licence to an established company to produce his invention.

Manx Bar

The body of barristers specially qualified to practise in the independent legal system of the Isle of Man.

mare clausum *(Lat.)*

An area of sea closed to general shipping by virtue of the claim of a particular country to exercise jurisdiction over it.

marginal note

A note appearing at the side of each section of a Bill being considered by Parliament; it does not form part of the Bill itself.

marine insurance contract

A contract of indemnity by which an underwriter agrees to cover another person (the insured) in respect of any losses to ship or cargo.

maritime lien

A right over a ship to secure a debt or claim against its owners.

market

A meeting-place where potential vendors and purchasers come together for the purpose of dealing in goods or services.

market overt

Special protection for purchasers of goods of doubtful ownership in certain recognised markets in England and Wales, or any shop in the City of London.

market price

In City parlance, the price at which stocks and shares have been bought and sold on the Stock Exchange; generally, the level of price which goods or services command at a given time.

marksman

Someone who cannot write his name, but who is obliged to sign by marking an X.

marriage brokage contract

An agreement to arrange or bring about a particular marriage, which is contrary to public policy, and therefore void.

marriage duty

An assessed tax imposed in 1695 on the husband of every marriage where neither was in receipt of alms. It was on a sliding scale according to the social position of those involved, and was abolished in 1706.

marshalling the assets

The order of priority for the payment of a dead person's debts and legacies where his property is not sufficient to meet them all.

marriage settlement

A formal agreement by one or both parties to a marriage to bring certain property into their joint assets.

martial law

A condition under which ordinary laws are suspended, and a country becomes governed by military tribunals.

master and servant

An expression (now slightly archaic) describing the relationship of employer and employee.

Master of the Crown Office

A Master of the Queen's Bench Division of the High Court who supervises the Crown Office Department.

Master of the Rolls

The President of the Court of Appeal (Civil Division). He also supervises the admission of candidates to the Roll of Solicitors.

maternity allowance

A state benefit payable to an expectant mother who has made certain National Insurance contributions.

maternity grant

A non-contributory state benefit payable to a woman who is expecting or has recently given birth to a baby.

maternity leave

An entitlement to paid leave for a woman who stops work in order to have a baby, and who has previously worked for the qualifying period.

maternity rights

The rights of a female employee to payment of wages or salary during and after pregnancy, and subsequently to be re-employed.

mate's receipt

A receipt for goods carried by a vessel, signed by the ship's mate after loading, and later exchanged for the bill of lading.

matrimonial offence

One of the former grounds for divorce such as desertion, cruelty or adultery, now evidence of irretrievable breakdown of marriage.

matrimonial relief

An order of a court for divorce, nullity, judicial separation, or a finding of presumed death of a husband or wife.

maturity

The time at which a payable order becomes due for payment.

Mayor's and City of London Court

The court for the City of London with county court jurisdiction.

mead
> An alcoholic drink made by dissolving honey in water, adding herbs and spice, and fermenting with yeast.

measure of the General Synod
> A resolution of the GENERAL SYNOD (q.v.), which has the force of law.

Mechanical Copyright Protection Society (M.C.P.S.)
> The organisation responsible for the administration of the MECHANICAL RIGHT (q.v.) in copyright musical works.

mechanical lighter duty
> An indirect tax imposed on any mechanical contrivance intended to produce a spark or flame.

mechanical right
> In copyright, the right to make a sound recording of a musical work.

medical inspection
> A formal examination of a wife which takes place in nullity proceedings, where it is claimed that there has been a failure to consummate the marriage.

Mediterranean pass
> A pass formerly issued on behalf of the Admiralty to any ship under a British flag sailing for a destination where capture by Barbary pirates was possible. By agreement with the Barbary states it afforded protection against piracy, but it was discontinued in 1853.

members' voluntary winding up
> A voluntary winding up of a company with a statement that a majority of its directors consider that it will be able to pay its debts in full.

memorandum clause
> A clause in a policy of marine insurance excluding certain goods specially liable to damage from the operation of the clause in certain circumstances.

memorandum of association
>A document relating to a company setting out its name, objects and capital, and any limitation on its members' liability.

mens rea *(Lat.)*
>A guilty intention for the purposes of criminal law.

mercantile agent
>A person who in the normal course of his business as an agent has authority to sell goods, consign goods for sale, purchase goods, or raise money on their security.

mercantile law
>Another name for commercial law.

merchandise marks legislation
>Legislation prohibiting misleading descriptions of goods, services, accommodation and other facilities, now replaced by the TRADE DESCRIPTIONS LEGISLATION (q.v.)

merchant shipping law
>The branch of law which affects the rights and obligations of people operating in commercial navigation at sea.

mercy killing
>Popularly applied to cases where it is alleged that a person was killed in order to relieve suffering. This is not at present a defence to a criminal charge.

merger
>The combining of two or more undertakings to operate under the name of one of them, or under a new name.

mesne profits
>Income from land lost by one person during the time another person wrongfully remains in possession.

messuage
>In the law of property, a dwelling-house and any land attached to it.

Metropolitan Police
>   A branch of the police, operating in Greater London, directly under the control of the Home Secretary, whose Commissioner is appointed by the Crown.

Metropolitan Police Solicitor
>   A prosecuting solicitor employed in the office of the Solicitor for the Metropolitan Police.

Middle Temple
>   One of the four societies entitled to admit people to the rank of barrister by calling them to the Bar.

Midland and Oxford Circuit
>   One of the six circuits of the Bar of England and Wales.

military law
>   A special system of law to which members of the navy, army, and air force become subject on enlistment.

military salvage
>   The recovery from an enemy in wartime of captured vessels.

ministerial tribunal
>   A tribunal appointed by a minister or Government department to hear appeals from decisions of other tribunals or local authorities.

minister of state
>   A minister of the Government to whom special duties may from time to time be assigned.

minor
>   A person under the age of eighteen, formerly known as an infant.

minority
>   The state of being under the age of eighteen, once known as infancy.

minutes
>   The records of a company's GENERAL MEETINGS (q.v.) and of meetings of its directors and executive, which it is obliged to keep in prescribed form.

misbehaviour in public office

A criminal offence at common law committed by any public official who has acted in an irregular manner.

mischief rule

A rule for the interpretation of laws by the judges, by which they look for the mischief which that law was supposed to suppress.

misdemeanour

At one time a classification of less serious crimes, now abolished.

misfeasance

Something which has been done, but done badly, for example repair of the highway by a public authority, or the handling of a company's assets.

misjoinder

The improper or unnecessary joining of someone as a party to a legal action.

misprision

Some kind of neglect or oversight which is not given a more precise legal definition.

misprision of treason

The criminal offence of having knowledge of and concealing an act of TREASON (q.v.), without actually agreeing to take part in it.

misrepresentation

A false statement made to induce a person to enter a contract.

mistake in venue

The bringing of proceedings in the wrong court.

mitigation

Facts put before the court by a person guilty of a criminal offence (or by his representative on his behalf), hoping to excuse or diminish the seriousness of the offence.

mitigation of damage

> The principle that a person who has suffered from a wrongful act must take steps as soon as possible to reduce the possibility of any further damage.

mixed policy

> A policy of marine insurance in which a particular period of time and a particular voyage are specified.

M'Naghten Rules

> A set of rules for judges to apply in deciding whether or not a person charged with a criminal offence is insane.

mobility allowance

> A state benefit payable to someone who is virtually unable to walk due to physical disablement.

moiety

> A half, generally in the sense of a half share in some property.

Monetary Compensatory Amounts

> A feature of the Common Agricultural Policy of the Common Market, by which accounting for compensation payments is adjusted in line with currency fluctuations.

money bill

> A parliamentary measure relating to public finance, such as the annual Finance Act, which must be introduced in the House of Commons; it cannot be amended by the Lords, and may become law without their consent.

monogamy

> Marriage between one husband and one wife. To take more than one spouse at the same time is the offence of bigamy.

monomaniac

> A person whose general understanding is sound, but who suffers delusions about a particular subject. He maintains the right to make an effective will.

monopsonist

> A buyer of goods or services who is in a monopoly position.

Monroe Doctrine
> The principle under which the USA claimed the right to repel European influence in the affairs of the entire American continent.

moratorium *(Lat.)*
> An agreement to desist from taking action to enforce a debt for a certain period of time.

mortgage
> A transaction entered into by the owner of property by which he gives a security over his land in return for the money he borrows.

mortgage debenture
> A DEBENTURE (q.v.) by which some property of a company is pledged for the money which it borrows.

mortgagee
> One who lends money to a landowner who has put up his land as security.

mortgage of land
> Land tendered by its owner as security for a loan of money.

mortgagor
> A landowner who offers his land or property as security for a loan.

mortmain rule
> The former rule that a corporation or company could not acquire land; it has now been abolished.

most favoured nation (most favoured party)
> A principle of international trading agreements by which a state (or party) can claim the most favourable treatment which has been accorded to any other contracting state (or party).

moveable property
> Objects and chattels, as opposed to land.

movement certificates
Documentation for the purposes of export and import in Common Market countries, relating to origin and transit security.

multinational
A term applied to an organisation whose interests, operations and properties are spread across a number of states.

muniments
Documents giving evidence of a claim or entitlement.

murage
In former times, a toll levied on goods brought into a walled town for sale, the proceeds of which were devoted to the upkeep of the walls.

murder
The unlawful killing of a person where death follows within a year and a day of the injury.

musical work
A combination of melody and harmony or either of them, set down in writing and which may be protected by copyright.

muster roll
A book kept on board a registered British ship containing personal particulars of all persons on board.

mutatis mutandis *(Lat.)*
The necessary changes being made.

mute by the visitation of God
Where a person accused of a crime does not answer when asked by a court how he pleads, and it is uncertain whether he is capable of understanding the proceedings.

mute of malice
The finding where a person accused of a crime does not answer when asked by a court how he pleads, and it is decided that he is deliberately keeping quiet.

mutual will

A will made by two people in favour of each other, with an eventual gift to a third person on the death of the second of the two makers.

N

naming a member
> A finding by a speaker of the House of Commons that a Member of Parliament has misbehaved himself in some way.

nationality
> Membership of a state or nation governing an individual's political status and allegiance.

National Research and Development Corporation (N.R.D.C.)
> A government-supported organisation developing and exploiting inventions in both the public and private sectors.

naturalisation
> The grant of United Kingdom citizenship to a foreigner, at the discretion of the Home Secretary.

natural parents
> The man and woman whose sexual relationship has brought about the birth of a child.

natural persons
> Human beings, as opposed to companies (to which the law gives a form of personality).

nautical assesor
> A skilled expert in maritime matters who sits with a judge in Admiralty cases, to assist on points needing special skill.

necessaries

Goods suitable to the life style and needs of MINORS (q.v.) and mentally disordered persons.

necessity

Sometimes raised as a defence in criminal cases, rarely with success, and certainly not where the personal needs of the accused person was the only factor.

nec per vim nec clam nec precario *(Lat.)*

In order to establish a custom, the requirement that it must have existed neither by the use of force, nor secretly, nor under a revocable licence.

negligence

The breach by one person of his legal duty to take enough care not to cause injury to another person or to his property.

negotiability

The condition by which a document itself and all rights created under it can be transferred simply by delivery, or by delivery with endorsement. Examples are cheques and bills of exchange.

negotiable instrument

A document, all rights in which can be transferred simply by delivery, or delivery with endorsement, such as cheques or bills of exchange.

negotiorum gestio *(Lat.)*

The supervision or conduct of the affairs of another person.

negrohead

A variety of tobacco made up and twisted into rolls resembling the head of a negro.

nemo dat quod non habet *(Lat.)*

The principle that no one can pass on to another person a better title or right than he himself enjoys.

nemo debet bis puniri *(Lat.)*
   The rule that no one can be subjected to a double punishment; a man may not be punished twice for the same offence.

nett running yield
   The annual return from an investment expressed as a percentage of its market price or cost, after deduction of income tax at the standard rate.

nett profit
   The profit remaining after deduction of all expenses.

neutral spirit
   Alcohol so devoid of characteristics that there is nothing to distinguish it from any other type of pure spirit.

newspaper duty
   A stamp duty on newspapers, first levied in 1712, but abolished in 1855.

next friend
   A responsible person appointed to bring an action in court on behalf of some other person, such as a child, who is not able to deal with the matter on his own account.

nexus *(Lat.)*
   Link; connection.

no case to answer
   A submission which can be made by the defence in criminal cases at the end of the prosecution case. If successful, the case is dismissed without the defendant having to give evidence, or put his case.

nolle prosequi *(Lat.)*
   A prerogative power exercised by the Attorney-General to halt more serious criminal prosecutions.

nominal capital
   The nominal amount of share capital which a limited company is permitted to issue by its MEMORANDUM OF ASSOCIATION (q.v.). Known also as authorised capital.

nominal damages
> An award reflecting the view that any loss or damage is purely technical.

nominal value
> The face value of a security such as a company share.

nominee company
> A company formed generally for the purpose of holding shares in the name of another company, thereby concealing the name of the true owner of the shares.

nominee shareholder
> A person officially registered as the owner of shares, where they are in fact really owned by another person.

non-capital murder
> Murder punishable by life imprisonment, as opposed to death.

non-cohabitation clause
> A court order to the effect that one party to the marriage is no longer obliged to live with the other. It does not in itself amount to a divorce.

non compos mentis *(Lat.)*
> Not fully in possession of one's mental faculties.

non constat *(Lat.)*
> It is not certain.

non-consummation
> The absence of sexual intercourse between husband and wife, which can amount to a ground for annulling the marriage.

non-cumulative preference shares
> PREFERENCE SHARES (q.v.) which do not carry the entitlement to make good any default from previous years before ordinary shareholders receive a dividend.

non est factum *(Lat.)*
> A denial of responsibility such as for the execution of a document signed under duress or intoxication.

non-exclusive licence

An agreement under which one person acquires the right to use something protected by monopoly rights such as copyright or patents, but at the same time cannot prevent a similar right being granted to another person.

non-executive director

A member of the board of a company who is not full time, but who is included in order to contribute special expertise which his colleagues may not possess.

non-feasance

Something which needed to be done, but which has been completely omitted, particularly in relation to highway repairs.

non liquet *(Lat.)*

A declaration that in the absence of any governing rule, an issue is not clear, and cannot be decided.

non sequitur *(Lat.)*

A statement which is illogical or inconsistent.

non-suit

A formal decision by a judge that a person bringing a case has not proved it sufficiently to be allowed to continue.

non-voting shares

A category of ORDINARY SHARE (q.v.) in a limited company with restricted voting rights, in order to preserve the influence of the original shareholders.

Nordic Council

An association for mutual co-operation between the Scandinavian countries, including Iceland and the Faroes.

North Atlantic Treaty Organisation (NATO)

An agreement providing for mutual self-defence and security between most West European states, USA and Canada.

North-Eastern Circuit

One of the six circuits of the Bar of England and Wales.

Northern Circuit
One of the six circuits of the Bar of England and Wales.

Northern Ireland Bar
The body of barristers specially qualified to practise in the separate legal system of Northern Ireland.

Norwich Guildhall Court
A local court of ancient origin with limited jurisdiction in East Anglia to try civil cases. It was abolished in 1971.

nostrum
A medicine the composition of which is secret.

notary public
An official, often a solicitor, empowered to verify certain types of business documents, and to make particular records.

note of hand
An old-fashioned expression for a promissory note.

not guilty
The denial of the charge by a person accused of a criminal offence, by which the prosecution becomes obliged to prove its case; the verdict of a court or jury acquitting a person accused of a criminal offence.

not guilty by reason of insanity
A verdict available in criminal cases, where the person accused is found not to understand the nature and quality of his acts. It has the status of an acquittal, but the person so found may appeal against it.

notice of motion
The means by which a Member of Parliament indicates his intention to introduce a matter to the business of a particular day.

notice of opposition
The procedure by which an application for a patent may be contested.

not proven

An intermediate verdict available in criminal courts in Scotland, but not in England and Wales. Its effect is that while the person accused has not established his innocence beyond all reasonable doubt, there is not enough evidence to find him guilty.

notice of abandonment

In policies of marine insurance, a notice which must be given to UNDERWRITERS (q.v.) on the abandonment of a ship.

notice in lieu of distringas

In share dealings, a notice given by someone having an EQUITABLE INTEREST (q.v.) in the shares of a company, holding up the transfer of shares registered in the name of another person.

noting

A statement appended to a dishonoured bill of exchange noting the fact of dishonour.

noting junior

A barrister instructed to assist a more senior barrister in a particular case by taking a note of the proceedings. He does not normally address the court.

notorial act

Something which can only be carried out by a NOTARY PUBLIC (q.v.)

not under command

An expression used to signify a vessel which is not under control.

nova causa interveniens *(Lat.)*

Something placed independently between the original action of the person against whom a case is brought, and the damage complained of.

novation

The substitution of a new agreement for one which was already in existence.

novelty

The degree of originality essential to the grant of a patent for a new invention.

novus actus interveniens *(Lat.)*

A new act by a third party which comes between the original action of the person against whom a case is brought, and the damage complained of. It breaks the chain of responsibility for negligence.

nudum pactum *(Lat.)*

An agreement not having any legal effect.

nuisance

A TORT, which may be a PUBLIC NUISANCE (q.v.) or PRIVATE NUISANCE (q.v.)

nullity

The situation under which a marriage is held never to have been effective, for example because of one partner's impotence.

nullum tempus occurit Regi *(Lat.)*

Time never runs against the Crown.

nuncupative will

An oral declaration in the nature of a will exceptionally regarded by the law as valid in the case of servicemen on active service, and sailors at sea.

O

oath

A soleman declaration sworn on the basis of an individual's religious beliefs.

oath of allegiance

The swearing of allegiance to the monarch, which must be performed by every Member of Parliament.

obiter dicta *(Lat.)*

Observations made by a judge in the course of his judgement which are not fundamental to the principle on which he is passing judgement.

objection in point of law

In formally pleading a case, an admission of facts alleged, coupled with an objection that they do not give rise to a case at law.

objects clause

A statement in the memorandum of association of a company of the main purposes for which it exists.

obligor

A person bound under the terms of a BOND (q.v.) to pay money or to carry out some act.

obscene play

The performance or direction of an obscene play in public constitutes a criminal offence.

obscene publication

The publication of any material which is obscene, in that it tends to deprave or corrupt, is a criminal offence.

obstructing the police

To obstruct a police officer who is acting in the course of his duty is a criminal offence.

obtaining credit by fraud

A former crime involving the obtaining of a pecuniary advantage by deception, now replaced by the general law relating to theft.

obtaining property by deception

The criminal offence of getting hold of another person's property, with the intention of permanently depriving him of it.

obviousness

A ground for opposing the grant of a patent, and contradicting its claim to be new.

occasional licence

A special licence to sell excisable goods such as alcohol and tobacco on special occasions at prescribed places.

occupation

In international law, a method of acquiring territory not already forming part of the dominions of any state.

occupier's liability

The duty of care owed by an occupier of premises to lawful visitors who are entering them.

offence triable either way

A criminal offence which can be heard either summarily by magistrates (justices of the peace), or on indictment before a Crown Court.

offer of amends

A defence to an action for defamation, where it can be shown that a suitable correction and apology was made in respect of words uttered innocently, and that this was accepted by the person defamed.

offeree

> The person to whom the offer of a contract is made.

offeror

> The person making an offer of a contract.

office of profit

> A Crown appointment which disqualifies the holder from membership of the House of Commons.

Official Receiver

> An official who assumes responsibility for the protection of a debtor's property on the making of a RECEIVING ORDER (q.v.)

Official Referee

> A circuit judge designated to hear cases involving lengthy consideration of complex documents and accounts.

official reference

> The citation of an Act of Parliament by reference to the session in which it was passed, and its number or chapter.

official secrets

> Classified information confidential to the administration of the state, the unauthorised disclosure of which constitutes a criminal offence.

Official Solicitor

> An officer of the Supreme Court of Judicature who acts for people committed to prison for contempt of court, and for litigants who are of unsound mind.

old-style committal

> A detailed examination by magistrates of the evidence of a serious crime in order to establish whether the matter should be tried by a jury.

omnibus credit

> Credit facilities granted to a shipper of good financial standing allowing drawings against the security of a general lien on the shipper's goods.

one parent benefit

A state benefit payable to single parents or others bringing up a child on their own.

op. cit. (opere citato) *(Lat.)*

Where found in a passage in a book, it means 'in the work previously referred to.'

open account policy

A form of bad-debt insurance, by which each invoice not met is written off the total amount insured.

open cheque

An uncrossed cheque which may be paid over the counter to the person holding it, or the person in whose favour it is drawn, or to a person to whom it has been transferred by endorsement.

opening a cheque

The act of nullifying a restrictive crossing on a cheque, so that it can be cashed across the counter of a bank.

open policy

A policy, generally of marine insurance, which does not specify the value of the subject-matter which has been insured.

operative mistake

A mistake of fact, as opposed to a mistake of law.

opposed business

Matters in the House of Commons to which objection is taken.

option

The right to bring into force a binding contract at some time in the future.

ordeal

A form of deciding a matter judicially in the Middle Ages by means of a physical test, such as the holding of a hand in fire.

Order Book

A day-to-day list of all House of Commons business for the remainder of the Parliamentary term.

Order Paper
> A printed list of business to be taken each day in the House of Commons.

Order in Council
> A form of DELEGATED LEGISLATION (q.v.) made by the Sovereign in Council under authority of an Act of Parliament, generally issued without further reference to Parliament.

Orders
> A form of DELEGATED LEGISLATION (q.v.) made by Ministers, usually requiring submission to Parliament prior to coming into force.

ordinary resolution
> A decision passed at the meeting of a company by the majority of the people present who are entitled to vote.

ordinary revenue of the Crown
> Income which the sovereign once received from Crown lands and BONA VACANTIA (q.v.) Now replaced by the CIVIL LIST (q.v.)

ordinary shares
> The category of shares in a limited company which is entitled to the balance of assets and profit remaining after the payment of dividends on preference shares.

Organisation for Economic Co-operation and Development (O.E.C.D.)
> An international organisation devoted to the expansion of world trade and the raising of living standards.

original evidence
> The testimony of a witness who speaks to facts from his own knowledge.

original precedent
> A decision of a court which creates and applies a new rule.

originating application
> A means of commencing proceedings in the county court.

originating summons
> A method of commencing a non-contentious procedure in the Chancery Division of the High Court.

ostensible authority
> Powers within the apparent scope of an agent's authority.

outlawry
> In ancient times, the expulsion of a wrongdoer from the community; his property became forfeit, and he could be pursued and killed.

outport
> Every customs port in the United Kingdom, apart from the Port of London.

output tax
> The charge of **VALUE ADDED TAX** (q.v.) to the price of goods or services by the person making the supply, and paid by the person receiving the supply.

outs
> Formerly applied to casks of wine which had leaked during an inward voyage.

outward processing
> The exportation of goods from the United Kingdom for processing abroad and eventual return to this country. It attracts certain relief from duty.

overproof
> The strength of spirit of which the specific gravity is less than that of proof spirit.

overreaching
> A principle of property law which allows obstacles in the way of a purchaser to be overcome, if the obstacle is one of a defined class, and the purchase money is paid to those entitled to receive it.

overriding commission
> The commission paid by a company to a main UNDERWRITER (q.v.) for arranging further contracts to lay off part of his liability with other people.

overriding interest
> A right in land not recorded on a land certificate.

overseas company
> A company with a place of business outside Great Britain.

Overseas Office
> A department under the authority of the Clerk to the House of Commons.

overt act
> An act manifesting criminal intent and tending towards the carrying out of a criminal objective.

P

package

A right granted by charter to the City of London in 1641 to examine and pack goods brought there by foreigners for export. The rights were bought out in 1833.

packet boat

A vessel used for the conveyance of passengers by water within the United Kingdom.

paid-up capital

The total amount which has been paid up on the issued share capital.

paid-up licence

An agreement under which a person taking a licence can make as much use of it as he wishes for a lump sum, as opposed to a royalty payment.

paid-up policy

A policy of assurance on which no further premiums are due to be paid.

paid-up policy value

The amount to which the sum assured on a life policy would be reduced if a re-arrangement were sought with no further payment.

pairing

The procedure in the House of Commons by which a member

of Parliament who wishes not to attend makes an arrangement with a Member from the other side of the House who wishes to do the same.

Palatine Court of Durham
A court which formerly exercised jurisdiction in chancery matters in the county of Durham; it is now merged into the High Court.

Palatine Court of Lancaster
A court which formerly exercised jurisdiction in chancery matters in the county of Lancashire; it is now merged into the High Court.

pardon
The right of the Crown to order the annulment of sentence and conviction, reduction of sentence, or substitution of another form of penalty.

pari passu *(Lat.)*
Without difference or distinction between two or more objects, persons or things.

Parliamentary agent
A person who looks after the process of taking private bills through Parliament. Generally a solicitor in private practice.

Parliamentary Bar
The group of barristers who specialise in appearing before committees of Parliament.

Parliamentary Counsel
See Parliamentary Draftsman.

Parliamentary Draftsman
A member of the Government Legal Service with special responsibility for drawing up Bills and Acts of Parliament.

Parliamentary privilege
The freedoms of a Member of Parliament are freedom of speech and freedom from arrest for debt, or for jury service.

Parliamentary sovereignty

The principle that Parliament can pass any law that it chooses, and that there is no law which cannot be altered by Parliament.

Parole Board

A panel advising the Secretary of State on the early release of prisoners before the conclusion of their full sentence.

participating policy

A policy of life assurance, under which the person assured receives a share of the issuing company's profits.

participating preference shares

PREFERENCE SHARES (q.v.) in a category which provides that, after paying a dividend to preference and ordinary shareholders, the participating shares will receive favourable treatment in any further distribution.

particular average

A maritime loss arising from a danger insured against, other than a GENERAL AVERAGE loss (q.v.)

particular charges

In marine insurance, extra expense incurred for the protection of whatever has been insured.

particular lien

The right of a person in possession of goods to retain them until any debts incurred in connection with those goods have been met. An example would be a tradesman who has carried out repairs on goods.

partition

The right of a joint tenant to call for the sale of the property, so that each joint tenant may take his specified share.

partner

A person who has entered into the relations of a PARTNERSHIP (q.v.)

partnership

A relationship existing between persons carrying on a business in common with a view to profit.

partnership at will

A partnership without any fixed term, or one which carries on after the time originally set for bringing it to an end.

part performance

A remedy where one person has performed part of a contract normally requiring written evidence, but oral evidence exists, and it would be fraudulent of the other person to take advantage of the absence of writing.

party

Usually applied to a person involved on one side or the other in a civil case.

party and party costs

An amount payable by the unsuccessful party to a civil action to the successful party, allowing all essential charges incurred by the other side, but not unnecessary ones.

passage

For the purposes of maritime law, a single trip, either outwards or home.

passenger's baggage

The clothing and personal effects of a passenger.

passim *(Lat.)*

Throughout a book (relating to a reference in it).

passing a dividend

The action of a company which decides not to pay a dividend at a time when it would normally be due.

passing off

A civil action by one person whose trade has been damaged by another person who used misleading trade descriptions to enhance customers' interest in his own product.

passport
    A document giving details of a person's nationality and identity for use when travelling abroad.

patent
    A grant of monopoly made by the state to an inventor giving him for a fixed period the sole right of manufacturing or applying the invention.

patent agent
    A member of the profession which engages in the application for and obtaining of patents in respect of inventions.

Patent Examiner
    An official whose duty is to check applications for patents, and to search for previous similar inventions.

patent of addition
    An improvement or modification of a patented invention which is granted as a modification of the original patent.

patent number
    The serial number accorded to a patent for filing purposes when an application is granted.

Patent Office
    The office to which an application for a patent should be made within the United Kingdom

patent specification
    The detailed description of an invention in respect of which a patent is claimed.

Patents Court
    A branch of the Chancery Division set up to hear patent cases, with a specialist judge and advisers.

patient
    A person suffering from a mental disorder who is subject to certain disabilities at law.

patrial
> A person who enjoys the right to live in the United Kingdom because of his close association with this country.

pavage
> In former times, a toll charged on goods brought into a town for sale, and devoted to the upkeep of the roads there.

pawn
> A delivery of goods or the documents of title relating to them as security for making a loan or the carrying out of an obligation.

pawnbroker
> A person who keeps a shop for the taking of goods as security for money advanced on them.

pawnee
> The person to whom goods or the documents of title relating to them are delivered as security for the payment of a debt or the carrying out of an obligation.

pawnor
> The person who delivers goods or the documents of title to them as security for the payment of money he has borrowed or the carrying out of an obligation he is under.

P.A.Y.E.
> The Pay As You Earn system, under which income tax is deducted from wages and salaries by employers, and the balance paid nett to employees.

payee
> The person to whom payment is directed to be made, in an order such as a cheque or a bill of exchange.

paying public domain
> A suggested form of funding for the arts, by levying a royalty on the use of works in which copyright has already expired.

payment of honour
> Where someone such as a banker has refused to pay on a bill

of exchange drawn on him, someone else may step in and make payment for the honour of the person whose bill has been dishonoured.

payment into court
A device open to the defence in civil claims. If a sum of money is paid into court, and the judge does not award damages of a larger amount, the claimant cannot receive any costs after the date of payment into court.

pedlar
An itinerant trader going from door to door offering goods for sale.

peine forte et dure *(Fr.)*
A medieval procedure by which a person accused of a criminal offence could either admit it or be crushed to death.

pendente lite *(Lat.)*
While litigation or court proceedings are pending.

penology
The scientific study of the sentencing of criminals.

peppercorn rent
A rent which is purely nominal.

per *(Lat.)*
With reference to a statement by a judge, 'in the opinion of'.

per curiam *(Lat.)*
In the view of the court.

peremptory challenge
An objection to a juror made without giving a reason for it.

perfect entry
A declaration of goods for customs purposes in final and complete form.

performance
The complete fulfilment of a contract.

performance bond
> A sum of money put up as a guarantee by a person undertaking a job under contract.

performing right
> The right to forbid (or allow) the performance of a work subject to copyright control.

Performing Right Society (P.R.S.)
> The organisation responsible for the administration of the PERFORMING RIGHT (q.v.) in copyright musical works in Britain.

Performing Right Tribunal
> An independent tribunal which sits to fix the rate in disputes over the performing and broadcasting rights in musical works and records.

periodical payments
> A form of order for maintenance which may be made in matrimonial cases.

perils
> An expression used in insurance contracts to describe those eventualities which are covered, and those which are excluded.

perils of the sea
> Applied in contracts of marine insurance to accidents arising in the course of navigation, as opposed to inevitable occurences.

per incuriam *(Lat.)*
> By carelessness.

perjury
> The wilful making of a false statement by someone who has taken the oath as a witness in judicial proceedings.

perpetual debentures
> DEBENTURE CAPITAL (q.v.) issued on the basis that the amount lent to the company is repayable only in the event of its winding up, or some other condition.

perpetual injunction
> A court order of permanent effect, by contrast with one granted only until the trial of the main issue.

perpetual succession

The process by which a corporation or company continues its identity, despite the death or withdrawal of some members.

per pro (p.p., per procurationem) *(Lat.)*

An indication that the person who actually signs a document is signing on behalf of another person. A signature 'per pro' indicates a limited authority on the part of the signatory, who may not exceed the powers granted by the person on whose behalf he signed.

personality

The quality of existence in the eyes of the law. An action can only be brought by or against a real person or a body enjoying legal personality. An example of such a body would be a company, which acquires its personality by incorporation.

per quod *(Lat.)*

By virtue of which.

per se *(Lat.)*

On its own.

persona *(Lat.)*

A person or thing having PERSONALITY (q.v.) in the eyes of the law.

personal chattels

Objects such as household goods and clothing, as opposed to objects used for business purposes.

personal property

The section of the law concerned with rights over chattels or physical objects, as opposed to land.

personal representative

In relation to a will or succession to property, an EXECUTOR (q.v.) or an ADMINISTRATOR (q.v.)

personal service

The act of delivering formal legal documents personally to a party to proceedings, generally by a process-server such as a bailiff.

personalty
Personal property in the nature of chattels, as opposed to land. Not to be confused with PERSONALITY (q.v.)

per stirpes *(Lat.)*
By the roots. In wills or intestate succession it means that property is divided equally among surviving children; where a child has died, his share is divided among his children.

persuasive precedent
A decision of a court which another court is not absolutely bound to follow, but which it will treat with considerable respect.

perverse verdict
A decision of a jury which no group of reasonable people, properly directed by a judge, could have found on the evidence. It rarely succeeds as a ground for appealing.

perversion of the course of justice
A criminal offence at common law committed by someone tampering with the machinery of the courts, for example by interfering with the evidence.

per subsequens matrimonium *(Lat.)*
By subsequent marriage. A technique by which illegitimate children may be made legitimate.

petition
A method of commencing divorce proceedings; also certain types of case in the Chancery Division of the High Court.

petitioner
A person applying for relief under a divorce or other petition.

petty asizes
In medieval times, twelve freeholders of a district charged with deciding a dispute over possession of property.

Petty Sessional Division
The area or locality covered by a particular magistrates' court.

petty sessions
> Magistrates' courts, which hear less serious criminal cases (those which are not triable by a jury).

Phonographic Performance Limited (P.P.L.)
> The organisation responsible for collection of payments for the broadcasting use and public performance of gramophone records.

picketing
> The act of attempting by peaceful persuasion during an industrial dispute to influence a person either to work or not to work.

pilfering
> An expression popularly used to describe the unlawful removal of individual items, as opposed to the removal of an entire package.

pilot
> A person not forming part of the crew of a ship who is at some stage given control of its movements.

pilotage
> Fees levied for acting as a PILOT (q.v.)

pimp tenure
> A medieval right to hold land, in return for maintaining women for the king's pleasure.

pipe of wine
> A measure of 126 gallons of wine.

piracy
> Robbery, violence or murder committed at sea by people not acting under the lawful authority of any country.

plaint
> File reference for a case brought in the county court.

plaintiff
> A person who brings an action in civil law.

plaint note
> A document issued by a county court to a person who is commencing a case there.

plankage
> A fee levied on ships in harbour for the use of planks while loading or unloading cargoes at the dockside.

planning permission
> The sanction which must be obtained from the appropriate planning authority for the material alteration of the existing use of land or buildings.

plantation duties
> Customs duties originally imposed in 1673 on goods exported from the English colonies in America for destinations other than England.

plant seeds and varieties
> Legislation now protects a form of property right belonging to hybridists and plant breeders who develop new strains in the horticultural and agricultural world.

plea
> The response made by a person accused of a criminal offence when asked by a court whether or not he admits it.

pleadings
> Written statements delivered by both sides to a civil case setting out the arguments each will be putting forward at the trial.

plea of the Crown
> In medieval times, a case in which the king was technically interested, and which was triable by his judges.

plea of the jurisdiction
> A contention by a person accused of a criminal offence that he has already been found not guilty of the charge.

pledge
> The delivery of goods or the documents of title relating to them as security for a loan or the carrying out of an obligation.

pledgee

> The person to whom goods or the documents of title relating to them are delivered as security for the payment of money or the carrying out of an obligation.

pledger

> The person who delivers goods or the documents of title relating to them as security for the payment of money or the carrying out of an obligation.

plene administravit *(Lat.)*

> In an action against a dead person's estate, a defence by his PERSONAL REPRESENTATIVE (q.v.) that there is no property belonging to the dead person which can meet the claim.

plenipotentiary

> For the purposes of international law, an official acting on behalf of a state who does not have the full powers of head of state.

Plimsoll Line

> A line painted on the side of a ship to indicate the level to which it can safely be loaded.

police court

> A term popularly applied to a magistrates' court. Its use is not officially encouraged.

policy

> The principal document embodying a contract of insurance or assurance.

political uniform

> The wearing of a political uniform is a criminal offence unless permission has been obtained from the police authorities.

poll

> A procedure for cancelling or confirming a vote taken on a show of hands at a meeting of a company. It is open to any member present to demand a poll.

polygamous marriage
> A marriage entered into under a system of law which permits a spouse to take more than a single partner in wedlock.

pontage
> Tolls levied in former times on goods passing over a bridge.

pool betting duty
> A tax charged on all forms of betting by pools, and bets made at fixed odds with a bookmaker.

portage dues
> Former rights enjoyed by the Corporation of London to carry all goods between the River Thames and the premises of foreign merchants in London. Parliament bought them out in 1833.

port authority
> The body responsible for the management and maintenance of the area of a port.

portion
> The gift of money or property to a child by a parent or someone acting as such in order to provide for the child's future establishment in life.

port of adjudication
> The port to which a captured vessel is taken in a country with which its owners' state is at war.

port of registry
> The port at which a ship is registered, and to which she is regarded as belonging.

port risk policy
> In marine insurance, a policy under which cover ends as soon as the vessel leaves its moorings on a new voyage.

port wine
> A description which in the United Kingdom may only be applied to wines produced in Portugal.

possession
> Physical control exercised over a particular article which excludes other people from the same control of the article.

possessory lien

> The right of someone in possession of another person's property to keep it or control it until his claims against the owner of the property are satisfied.

postal packet

> Any article sent by post.

postal packet offences

> The sending of obscene or prohibited material through the post, which constitutes a criminal offence.

postal service

> The act of sending formal legal documentation by post to the address of a person's solicitor, or if he has none, to his last known address.

post-dated cheque

> A cheque bearing a date later than the day of issue, in order to delay payment, and usually to allow time for payment in of funds to meet it.

post entry

> A form of customs entry supplementary to the main entry made to adjust an undercharge of duty.

post horse duty

> An assessed tax levied first in 1779 at a rate per mile on any horse let for hire by the mile. It was administered by tollgate keepers, but abolished in 1869.

post mortem *(Lat.)*

> Generally, 'after death'; in particular, the medical examination of a corpse.

post nuptial settlement

> An agreement after a wedding by both partners to a marriage to bring specified property into their joint control.

post obit bond

> A personal security by which a borrower agrees to pay a lender a larger sum than the amount borrowed, to be paid on the death of another person from whom the borrower expects to inherit.

practising certificate
> A solicitor may not practise without obtaining annually a certificate from the Law Society.

praecipe *(Lat.)*
> Formerly, the document filed to start a case in the county court.

praemunire *(Lat.)*
> An ancient order to a sheriff to warn someone to appear before the king's council.

pratique
> Communication between the crew of a ship arriving from abroad and the inhabitants of a port, once it has been established that there was no sickness on the voyage.

preamble
> The introductory words setting out what an Act of Parliament is intended to achieve, but not forming part of the Act itself, nor available for use in its interpretation.

precatory trust
> A form of trust arising where a person gives property to another person, and expresses a wish that it be dealt with in a particular way.

precedent
> See JUDICIAL PRECEDENT. Also a form of words used as a model in drafting documents.

pre-emption clause
> A clause in the articles of a private limited company insisting on the offer of any shares for sale being made in the first place to existing members of the company.

preference
> The right to pay any creditor in preference to other creditors of equal standing.

preference shares
> Shares of a limited company having preferential status in

respect of a dividend, and the protection of capital if the company is wound up.

preferential debt

A debt of a bankrupt enjoying a high priority for payment out of any assets, for example a workman's wages.

pregnancy per alium

In matrimonial law, the condition of being pregnant by a man other than one's husband.

pre-preferential debts

Debts of a bankrupt enjoying a particularly high priority for payment out of any assets.

preferment of a bill of indictment

The putting forward of an indictment alleging a serious criminal offence against someone.

premium

(1) A payment under an insurance policy.

(2) A payment made to purchase a lease.

prerogative writ

Means by which an aggreived person can seek judicial enquiry into actions which have prejudiced him. An example is the writ of HABEAS CORPUS (q.v.)

prescriptive writ

A right which comes to be recognised in law where it can be shown to have existed openly and without dispute over a long period.

Press Gallery

A section in both Houses of Parliament where journalists may sit.

presumption

A fact assumed or taken for granted by the law.

presumption of advancement

The presumption that an actual purchaser of property in

another's name intends to benefit the nominal purchaser, rather than to create a trust in favour of himself.

presumption of death
The situation where one party to a marriage has not been heard of for 7 years, and the other party has no reason to believe that he or she is still living. If it cannot be shown that the absent person is alive, a divorce can be obtained.

presumption of legitimacy
The assumption made by the law that every child born to a married woman is legitimate.

presumption of life
A presumption of law that a person is considered to be living until the contrary is shown.

presumption of marriage
Where a marriage certificate has been looked for, but cannot be found, a valid marriage will be presumed by the law from the fact of co-habitation, until the contrary is proved.

presumptive charge
Estimated produce of materials employed in the brewing of beer or the distillation of spirits.

pre-trial review
A consideration by the court of matters which will arise in a long trial, in an effort to shorten proceedings, and save time and expense.

prevention of corruption
A branch of criminal law designed to prevent the illegal obtaining of advantage by the offer of a bribe, or an inducement given to advance a person's chances of obtaining a title or honour.

preventive detention
A form of punishment previously applied to persistent offenders.

price/earnings ratio

    The market price of a share expressed as the number of years' purchase of current earnings per share.

prima facie *(Lat.)*

    On the face of things; at first sight.

prima facie case

    Literally, a case at first sight. It is applied where the side making an allegation demonstrates enough to make the other side contest the issue, and thus defeats any counterclaim that there is no case to answer.

primage and average

    Fees customarily paid under a BILL OF LADING (q.v.) to the master of a ship.

primary evidence

    The best evidence available as a means of proof. An example would be an original document.

Prime Minister

    The leader of the political party commanding a majority in the House of Commons; the chief minister in the Government.

primogeniture

    The former right of the eldest son to inherit property, in the absence of a will. It is no longer applicable in England, except in relation to hereditary titles.

principal

    (1) The person on whose behalf an agent acts.

    (2) The original sum invested or advanced on a loan.

prior art

    The existing state of knowledge in a particular field of invention.

prisage (also butlerage)

    Wine formerly prised or taken by the King's Butler for the king's use from every ship bringing in wine.

prisoner
> A defendant or accused person in a criminal case who is remanded in custody. The use of the term is not encouraged at the present time.

prisoner at the bar
> The person in the dock who is accused of a criminal offence.

private bill
> A measure generally of local or particular interest, which passes through Parliament by a process differing from that for a PUBLIC BILL (q.v.)

Private Bill Office
> A department under the authority of the Clerk of the House of Commons, responsible for private bills.

private carrier
> A person who carries goods or persons for reward only occasionally, or under a special agreement.

private company
> A company which may not invite the public to subscribe for its shares; this limits its membership, and restricts the right to transfer its shares.

privateer
> A privately owned ship which is armed and engaged by a country at war to attack the vessels or territory of its enemies.

private effects
> Articles intended for the owner's private use, not intended for sale or gift to other people.

private international law
> The system of law governing disputes between individuals, which may involve the laws of more than one country.

private law
> Fields of law such as contract, tort and property, which control the rights and obligations of individuals between each other.

private member's bill

A bill introduced into the House of Commons by a Member of Parliament who is not a member of the Government.

private nuisance

An unauthorised use by one person of his property so as to cause damage to another's property, or disturb that other person's enjoyment of their property.

private prosecution

A prosecution brought by an individual on his own behalf, not through the police or other prosecuting authority.

privileged will

A will exceptionally allowed to be made by a minor (a person under the age of 18) if he is a sailor at sea, or a soldier or airman on active military service.

privity of contract

The rule that a person who is not one of those who actually made the contract cannot enforce any right or obligation contained in it.

prize

Something captured at sea from an enemy of the nation, for example an enemy ship.

prize court

A body set up at the commencement of hostilities to give judgement in the case of ships captured at sea.

prize crew

A group of seamen put on board a ship captured in time of war to sail it into a **PORT OF ADJUDICATION** (q.v.)

prize law

The procedures governing the capture of ships at sea in time of war.

probate

The formal proof of a will which must be applied for after the death of its maker.

probate in common form

The category of PROBATE (q.v.) which should be sought where there is no likelihood of any dispute.

probate in solemn form

The category of PROBATE (q.v.) which should be applied for if any chance exists that the validity of a will might be contested.

probation

An alternative to a prison sentence, by which the person so punished is placed under the supervision of a probation officer.

probation officer

A person trained in the supervision of criminal offenders outside the main prison system.

pro bono publico *(Lat.)*

For the public good or welfare.

process goods

Foreign goods imported for process or repair, and subsequent re-export.

process-server

A person such as a bailiff whose duties include the formal delivery of legal documents to a party to legal proceedings.

Procurator-Fiscal

A government-employed lawyer in the state prosecution service in Scotland who supervises police enquiries into more serious offences, prepares cases for trial, and conducts certain cases in court.

produce broker

A person who arranges for the purchase and sale of raw materials and commodities.

profit and loss acount

A statement which the directors of a company must put before a general meeting of its members each year.

profit à prendre *(Fr.)*

A right to take particular material from another person's land.

profits

Those assets of a company not representing capital or earmarked for meeting its liabilities, and which are available for distribution as dividends.

pro forma *(Lat.)*

'For form's sake'. In the case of an invoice, being for purposes of information, rather than an actual charge note.

pro hac vice *(Lat.)*

For this occasion only, standing in the place of the legal owners.

prohibited degrees

The ties of relationship which are too close to allow a marriage between a particular man and woman.

prohibited goods

Any goods the use or importation of which will prejudice the interests of the state; accordingly their use or import is forbidden.

prohibition

An order of the High Court to prevent a body or authority from acting unlawfully.

prohibitory injunction

A court order to prevent a wrongful act being carried out or continued.

promissory estoppel

A defence to an action over a contract by claiming that a person who had a right under that contract has agreed to suspend it.

promissory note

An unconditional written promise to pay either on demand or at some particular time in the future to either a particular person or his order, or to the person holding the promissory note.

promoter
A person who makes application to Parliament for a local or private Act to be passed.

proof
(1) The strength of alcoholic liquor as ascertained by hydrometer or other approved means.

(2) The evidence by which a fact alleged is sought to be established.

proof of debts
The procedure under which a creditor may make a claim for compensation from any assets in bankruptcy proceedings.

proof of evidence
A draft made by a solicitor of what it is hoped a witness will say in court.

proof of service
The formal establishment that documents have been properly left with a party to legal proceedings, either personally or by post.

property
The right of ownership over some item of material or human resources.

Property Register
One of the Land Registers containing descriptions of registered land by Ordinance Survey reference and postal address.

proposal form
A term used in insurance for the document on which the person proposing to take out a policy sets out details for the insurance company to consider.

proprietorship register
One of the Land Registers stating the type of title issued, and listing names and addresses of owners.

pro rata *(Lat.)*
In proportion.

prorogation of Parliament

The termination of a Parliamentary session on the authority of the Crown.

prospectus

An invitation to the public by a company to subscribe for shares or debentures.

prostitution

The act of indulging in sexual relations in return for payment.

pro tanto *(Lat.)*

In proportion to; to that extent.

protection of minorities

A general principle of company law by which it is sought to maintain a fair equilibrium between majority and minority shareholders.

protectorate

A territory placed under the protection of the Crown, but not forming part of the Crown's dominions.

pro tempore *(Lat.)*

For the time being.

protest

A formal statement drawn up by a notary public to record the fact that a bill of exchange has been dishonoured.

provable debts

Debts which a creditor is able to prove against the estate of a bankrupt.

provable non-provable debts

Debts which, although strictly capable of being taken into account or proved in bankruptcy proceedings, have been incurred in circumstances where a creditor loses his rights, generally because he has received notice of the situation.

provincial courts

The ecclesiastical courts of appeal of the Archbishops of York and Canterbury.

provisional certificate of registry
>A temporary certificate granted by a Registrar of Shipping other than the Registrar of the port of registration, or by a consular officer where a ship has become British while in a foreign port.

provisional collection of taxes legislation
>Legislation authorising the collection of taxes at new rates mentioned in a Budget resolution, until they are confirmed by Act of Parliament later in the session.

provisional liquidator
>An official appointed by the Court after presentation of a WINDING-UP PETITION (q.v.) and prior to the making of a final order, for the purpose of protecting the assets of the company concerned.

provisional order bill
>A bill introduced into Parliament to give legal effect to an order made by a Government Minister.

provisional specification
>An optional means of filing an early claim for patent protection for an invention, while the main claim is being prepared.

provocation
>In certain circumstances, a ground for reducing a charge of murder to manslaughter.

proximate cause
>A doctrine of marine insurance that the immediate and not the remote cause of a loss must be taken into account.

proxy
>A person appointed by a member of a company to attend a meeting of the company in his place, and to vote on his behalf.

publication
>The making known of a defamatory statement to a person other than the person at whom it was directed.

public bill
A measure introduced into Parliament which becomes an Act after passing through three readings, Committee and Report stages, in both Houses and receiving the Royal Assent, and which concerns a matter of public policy.

Public Bill Office
A department under the authority of the Clerk of the House of Commons dealing with public bills passing through the House.

public company
A company limited by shares which is not subject to the restrictions of a private company as to share transfer and which may invite the public to buy its shares. It must have a prescribed minimum share capital.

public domain
An intellectual creation or invention which is no longer subject to copyright or a patent, and therefore freely available for use, is said to be in the public domain.

public exhibition
A court appearance made by a debtor after the submission of his statement of affairs, or the expiry of the time limit for doing so.

public international law
The system of law governing relations between independent states.

public law
A classification covering constitutional, administrative and criminal law.

public lending right (P.L.R.)
A scheme to make limited payments to certain authors whose books are lent by public libraries.

public mischief
The concept of the general interest of the community at large, offences against which constitute crimes at law.

public nuisance
> An unlawful act or omission endangering public health, safety or comfort, or affecting some public right.

public stock
> Stock forming part of the National Debt, and transferable in the books of the Bank of England.

Public Trustee
> An official who can be appointed as a new or additional trustee by a court, the settlor, or anyone having the power of appointment.

puisne judge
> A Judge of the High Court. (Literally, a judge of lower rank).

puisne mortgage
> A legal mortgage not having the protection of deposit of title deeds.

pupillage
> A period of apprenticeship to be served by someone who has been called to the Bar, before he can hold himself out for independent practice as a barrister.

pur autre vie *(Fr.)*
> During another person's life.

purging contempt
> The act of clearing oneself from being in a state of CONTEMPT OF COURT (q.v.)

purser
> The officer on board a ship whose duty is to look after cargo, crew and passenger documentation.

putative father
> The person found by a court to be the father of an illegitimate child.

Q

qua *(Lat.)*
> In the capacity of.

quaere *(Lat.)*
> An indication that the correctness of a particular proposition should be questioned.

qualification shares
> The number of shares in a company which its articles may specify as a requirement to be held by any director.

qualified privilege
> A defence to an action for defamation where, if made without either spite or ill-will, the words complained of were uttered in certain circumstances where a special interest exists; an example would be as between a solicitor and his client.

quantum *(Lat.)*
> The amount, particularly in relation to an award of damages.

quantum meruit *(Lat.)*
> A claim for reasonable payment for work which has actually been carried out.

quantum valebant *(Lat.)*
> 'The amount which they were worth.'

quarantine
> The period during which an animal brought from abroad must be isolated before it can be released in the United Kingdom.

quarantine station
> The part of a port or airport approved for the importation of animals from abroad.

quartering
> The ancient punishment for people convicted of high treason, by which after death the body was divided into four quarters.

quarter sessions
> Former criminal court for less serious cases triable by jury. It has been replaced by the Crown Court.

quasi *(Lat.)*
> Having the appearance of.

quasi-contract
> A principle under which the law implies a promise on the part of one person to pay money to another.

quasi-derelict
> Applied to a vessel which has not been abandoned, but where the people left on board are unable to navigate in safety.

quasi-military organisation
> It is a criminal offence to belong to an organisation formed to usurp the functions of the police or armed forces, or organised to use force to promote a political objective.

Queen's Bench Division
> The section of the High Court dealing chiefly with civil disputes such as contract, negligence and defamation.

Queen's Consent
> The agreement of the Queen to Parliamentary consideration of any matter concerning Crown property or rights.

Queen's Counsel (Q.C.). (or King's Counsel)
> A senior barrister on whom that rank has been conferred by the Lord Chancellor. Now also drawn from successful

academics, legal authors, and employees in industry and the Government Legal Service, as well as from the practising Bar.

Queen's (King's) enemies

The armed forces of a country officially at war with the United Kingdom.

Queen's Proctor

An officer of the Crown with duties in probate and divorce cases. He is particularly concerned with concealment and collusion in divorce cases, although the office is of less importance than formerly.

Queen's Speech

The speech read by the Queen at the opening of each Parliamentary session, in which the Government's plans for legislation are outlined.

Queen's warehouse (King's warehouse)

A Crown Customs warehouse, for the storage of goods seized or detained by Customs and Excise.

question of law

A matter on which the judge should rule in a criminal trial, as opposed to questions of fact. There is wide scope for appeals on questions of law.

Question Time

The period of time set aside during business in the House of Commons, in which ministers answer questions put by Members of Parliament.

quia timet action

A case brought because someone is afraid of what might happen in the future.

quid pro quo *(Lat.)*

One thing in return for another; tit for tat.

qui facit per alium facit per se *(Lat.)*

He who does a thing by the action of another effectively does it himself.

qui prior est tempore, potior est jure *(Lat.)*
>   The principle that where equitable claims are equal, the first in time shall prevail.

quit rent
>   Formerly, a payment in order to rid oneself of certain feudal obligations or services.

quoad hoc *(Lat.)*
>   So far as this is concerned.

quod vide (q.v.) *(Lat.)*
>   Which see.

quominus *(Lat.)*
>   A device used by the old Exchequer Court to claim jurisdiction in civil disputes by alleging a fictitious debt due to the Crown.

quondam *(Lat.)*
>   Former; previous.

quorum *(Lat.)*
>   The minimum number who must be present before a meeting, particularly of the board of a company, can begin.

quoted company
>   A public limited company, the shares in which have been given a quotation on a recognised stock exchange.

R

racehorse duty

An assessed annual tax first imposed in 1784 on every horse starting in a race that year. Collected by the clerks of the course, it was abolished in 1874.

rackee of Turkey

An aromatic liqueur compounded in Turkey and neighbouring lands from spirits and certain spices.

racking

The process of drawing off wines and spirits from one cask or vessel into another.

rack rent

The highest sum which can be obtained as rental for a property of a particular value.

railway passenger duty

A former stamp duty first imposed in 1832 upon train passengers other than holders of cheap tickets.

rape

The criminal offence of having sexual intercourse with a female without her consent, by the use of force, fear or fraud.

rates

Local taxes on occupiers of property in the area of a local authority in order to raise revenue for its activities.

ratification
>   The act of confirming that something is legally binding.

ratio decidendi *(Lat.)*
>   The fundamental principle underlying a judgement or decision given by a judge.

raw spirits
>   Spirits which have not been rectified or compounded.

Reading Clerk
>   One of the permanent officials of the House of Lords.

readings
>   The three stages through which a Bill must pass on its way to becoming an Act of Parliament.

real property
>   The section of the law concerning itself with rights over land.

realty
>   Rights over land.

receipt
>   A written acknowledgement that a certain sum of money or an object has been received.

Receiver of Wreck
>   The COLLECTOR OF CUSTOMS AND EXCISE (q.v.) for a particular locality who acts on behalf of the Department of Trade in cases of wreck or salvage.

receiving order
>   An order making the OFFICIAL RECEIVER (q.v.) the guardian of a debtor's property, and halting all legal action against the debtor in respect of his debts.

receiving stolen property
>   A criminal offence, now known as handling stolen goods, by knowingly assisting in their retention, or making arrangements for their disposal.

recess

The period between two sessions of Parliament, when it is not sitting.

reciprocal enforcement

A system of enforcing in foreign countries which are party to an agreement with the United Kingdom the terms of maintenance agreements in this country.

recitals

Introductory phrases in a contract or agreement setting out the history and background to the transaction.

recognizance

A BOND (q.v.) or personal security given by a person to ensure the attendance of himself or another person at a court hearing.

reconstruction

Amending the capital structure of a company; or the transfer of its assets by one company to a new company, which adopts a new capital structure and the shareholders of the first company. The first company is wound up in the process.

recorder

A part-time judicial appointment given to barristers and solicitors, generally to test their suitability for appointment as circuit judge.

Recorder of London

The chief judge of the Central Criminal Court (Old Bailey).

record office

The location in which official records are kept for reference, in particular records of decided cases.

record piracy

The unauthorised manufacture of gramophone records the rights in which are owned by someone else.

rectification

The principle that where a document wrongly expresses the

intention of the people concerned, the court will allow it to be altered.

rectified spirits
> Pure spirits of the third extraction which have not been flavoured.

red bag
> A bag for carrying robes, traditionally presented by a Q.C. to a junior barrister who has given him useful assistance in a case. (see **BLUE BAG**).

reddendum *(Lat.)*
> A clause in a lease specifying the amount of rent reserved to the lessor.

redeemable debentures
> **DEBENTURE CAPITAL** (q.v.) the nominal amount of which the company is obliged to repay at a certain date, or in a prescribed way.

redeemable preference shares
> A category of **PREFERENCE SHARES** (q.v.) which may be bought back by a company if certain specified conditions are met.

reducing
> The process of reducing the strength of spirits by the addition of water.

reduction of capital
> The diminishing by a company of its share capital, a practice strictly forbidden without the authority of a court.

redundancy payment
> Payment made to a dismissed employee who has been continuously employed for a qualifying period of time.

re-exportation
> The exportation of goods which have previously been imported into the country, as opposed to the exportation of goods which originated in the United Kingdom.

re-examination
Questions put by an advocate to one of his own witnesses to re-establish his case after cross-examination of that witness by the other side.

refer to drawer
A comment made on a cheque by the bank on which it is drawn when dishonouring it.

reformation
A theory of criminology that the aim of a sentence should be the reform of the criminal concerned.

regent
A person appointed to act for a monarch who is under the age of eighteen.

regicide
The murder of a ruling king or queen.

registered club
A club occupying premises at which alcohol is sold, which must be registered with the justices of the peace for the area.

registered company
A corporation formed under the companies legislation.

registered debenture
DEBENTURE CAPITAL (q.v.) payable to a registered holder, and transferable in the same way as share capital.

registered office
The official location of a company, the address of which must be lodged with the Registrar of Companies.

registered security
Stocks or shares the title to which is evidenced by the issue of a certificate.

registered tonnage
Gross tonnage or cubic capacity of a ship expressed in tons of 100 cubic feet each, less approved deductions.

registered user
A person or company who has been registered as a licensee of a particular trade mark.

register of births, marriages and deaths
A register required since 1695 to be kept in every parish of all people born, christened, married or dying there.

Register of Business Names
A register formerly kept of firms, companies and partnerships trading under any style other than the name or names of the owner, or the corporate name of a company.

register of charges
A record which a company is obliged to keep of all liabilities secured on its assets, such as mortgages and charges. A general register is kept by the Registrar of Companies, and an individual one by each company.

register of directors and secretaries
A record which every company is obliged to keep giving personal particulars of each director and its secretary.

register of directors' interests
A record which a company is obliged to keep of the shareholdings of its directors and other relevant interests which they acquire.

register of members
A record of the members of a company which must be maintained, and its whereabouts notified to the Registrar of Companies.

Register of Patents
The official record of details relating to all patents for inventions.

register of substantial individual interests
A register which a limited company is obliged to maintain of the particulars of anyone acquiring 10% or more in nominal value of its relevant SHARE CAPITAL (q.v.)

Registrar

Court official (usually a solicitor) empowered to hear civil INTERLOCUTORY MATTERS (q.v.), other preliminary applications and some civil disputes.

Registrar of Companies

A public official whose duty is to record the incorporation of companies.

Registrar of Criminal Appeals

An official in charge of administrative matters in the Court of Appeal (Criminal Division), who organises the documentation and hearings.

Registrar of Shipping

The chief official of Customs and Excise in a port designated as a REGISTRY PORT (q.v.). He acts for the Department of Trade in matters relating to the registration of British ships.

Registrar of Trade Marks

The official at the PATENT OFFICE (q.v.) to whom application for the registration of a TRADE MARK (q.v.) must be made.

registry port

A port approved for the registration of British ships under the Merchant Shipping legislation.

regulated agreement

In consumer credit transactions, a CONSUMER CREDIT ARRANGEMENT (q.v.) or a CONSUMER HIRE AGREEMENT (q.v.), which is not an EXEMPT AGREEMENT (q.v.)

Regulation

A form of Common Market legislation binding as law within member countries without the need for any further legislation in that country.

Regulations

A form of DELEGATED LEGISLATION (q.v.) made by Ministers usually requiring submission to Parliament prior to coming into force as law.

rehabilitation
> A theory that a criminal who has served his sentence has paid his debt to society, and should be allowed to make a fresh start.

re-insurance
> The insuring by an underwriter of the whole or part of a risk he has himself insured, in order to relieve himself of the burden of it.

relation back
> The process by which the title of a trustee in bankruptcy over a bankrupt's property is backdated to a time three months prior to the debtor being adjudged bankrupt.

relator action
> A PREROGATIVE WRIT (q.v.) to prevent a public nuisance or an action in excess of powers.

release
> An abandonment of his outstanding rights by someone who has carried out his side of a bargain.

release on licence
> A scheme for the early release of prisoners before the conclusion of their sentence on the advice of the PAROLE BOARD.

relevant share capital
> Issued share capital of a class carrying the entitlement for the shareholder to vote at all general meetings.

remand
> An adjournment of a criminal case to a later date, the defendant being either remanded in custody or on bail.

remission
> The cancellation of part of a sentence of imprisonment, generally earned by good conduct.

remoteness of damage
> Damage which is too far removed from the original injury or loss to be the subject of a legal claim.

rent action

An action brought by a landlord against a tenant for arrears of rent.

rentcharge

A sum of money (other than rent) payable annually in respect of landed property.

rent rebates and allowances

Forms of state benefit payable to people who find difficulty in paying their full rent, whether or not they are in full-time employment. Rebates also exist for rates.

renunciation

The refusal by one person to carry out his side of a bargain, thus leading to a breach of contract.

renunciation letters

An annexation to an allotment of shares issued to the public, by which the person allotted the shares can renounce them in favour of another person.

repayment trader

A person registered for VALUE ADDED TAX (q.v.) who stands to receive more back from Customs and Excise than he is liable to pay.

replevin

An ancient action for unlawful detention of goods, long abolished.

reply

A written statement by the person making a claim in a civil case in response to a defence.

reporting restrictions

Restrictions on reporting by the media of certain court proceedings, particularly committals, which may be waived by the accused person.

Reports of Patent Cases

A series of law reports for cases involving INTELLECTUAL PROPERTY (q.v.)

Reports of Tax Cases
> A series of published decisions in cases relating.to specialised revenue matters.

representation
> Statement made to induce a person to enter a contract.

representative action
> Court proceedings taken by one person on behalf of another person or persons as well as himself.

reprieve
> The temporary suspension of the carrying out of the sentence imposed in a criminal case.

reputed ownership
> Applied to goods deemed to be under the control of a bankrupt with the consent of the owner, and therefore owned by a bankrupt.

requisitioned meeting
> A meeting of a company called at the request of the holders of not less than 10% of its paid-up voting capital.

request
> The document filed to start a case in the COUNTY COURT (q.v.)

requisition of title
> Inquiries on behalf of a prospective purchaser of a house to the representatives of the seller on matters about the title deeds of the property.

res *(Lat.)*
> Thing or matter.

res adiratae *(Lat.)*
> A early form of action to get back goods subject to unlawful detention. Succeeded by detinue, which in turn has been replaced by unlawful interference with goods.

resale loss policy

A form of bad-debt insurance, covering part of any loss where a supplier has taken back goods from an insolvent debtor.

resale price agreement

Formerly, a legitimate agreement among members of a trading sector to maintain prices at a particular level. Now generally unlawful, although books and newspapers are exempt.

rescission

The setting aside of a contract, or part of it.

reserve

That part of the profits of a limited company which have been held back from distribution to the shareholders by way of dividend.

reserve capital

Any section of the UNCALLED CAPITAL (q.v.) of a limited company, which has been stated by special resolution to be incapable of being called up, unless in a winding-up of the company.

reserve fund

That part of the profits of a limited company which have been held back from distribution to the shareholders, and invested in easily realisable assets.

res extincta *(Lat.)*

Something no longer existing.

res gestae *(Lat.)*

The facts in dispute.

residuary devisee

The person to whom all remaining land or property left under a will is given when specific gifts have been allotted.

residuary legacy

The gift by will of the balance of what is left after payment of expenses, death duties, debts and all other gifts.

res integra *(Lat.)*

A fresh point which is to be decided on its own facts.

res inter alios acta (alteri nocere non debet) *(Lat.)*

No one should be harmed by things which have taken place between other people.

res ipsa loquitur *(Lat.)*

Applied to actions in negligence where the facts of the wrongdoing are so obvious that they are said to speak for themselves and not require proof.

res judicata *(Lat.)*

The principle that a matter can no longer be questioned once a court has given its decision on it.

res nullius *(Lat.)*

Property having no owner.

resolution

A decision taken at a meeting of a company, which may be either SPECIAL, ORDINARY OR EXTRAORDINARY (q.v.)

resolution requiring special notice

A special decision relating to the appointment and removal of company directors and auditors, to which prescribed provisions for notice and advertisement apply.

res perit damno *(Lat.)*

The loss of a thing falls on its owner.

respondeat superior *(Lat.)*

The principle that a person in authority should assume authority.

respondent

In general, the other side in a case taken on appeal by an appellant; in particular, the person against whom a divorce petition is brought.

respondentia bond

A form of security pledging the cargo of a ship for the repayment of money borrowed for the purposes of a voyage.

restitutio in integrum *(Lat.)*

Restoration to the condition which existed previously.

restitution of conjugal rights

A form of matrimonial proceedings seeking an order that the spouse who left the other should return. It has now been abolished.

restitution of stolen property

A court may, where goods have been stolen, order their return to any person entitled to recover them, by means of a RESTITUTION ORDER (q.v.)

restitution order

A court order directing the return of property to a particular person.

restraint of princes

A limitation of liability inserted in contracts to guard against property being detained by official authority in foreign countries, against the owner's wishes.

restraint of trade

The restriction of competition between businesses, or of a person's freedom to follow his trade or profession.

Restrictive Practices Court

It sits to hear cases in which it is suggested that a particular method of doing business may distort trade or restrict fair competition.

resulting trust

A trust arising where a beneficiary predeceased someone who had set up a trust in their will, and the property is consequently held for the benefit of the personal representatives of the dead person.

res vendita *(Lat.)*

A thing which has been sold.

retainer

(1) The firm engagement of a barrister to act in a particular case, confirmed by a special payment.

(2) The right of a PERSONAL REPRESENTATIVE (q.v.) to pay a debt due to himself from the dead person before he pays other creditors of equal standing.

retirement by rotation

A procedure usually provided for in the ARTICLES OF ASSOCIATION (q.v.) of a company, by which one third of its directors retire by rotation at every annual general meeting, but may stand again for re-election.

retirement pension

The old age pension. It is a state benefit payable to a man over 65 or a woman over 60 who has retired from work.

retribution

A theory that the sentence imposed on a convicted criminal satisfies the feeling of society that guilt should be punished.

return day

The last day specified for the lodging of a particular document.

revenue

(1) The income of the state. In popular speech applied to matters relating to its collection and administration.

(2) Income in general.

revenue reserve

That part of any RESERVE (q.v.) held back by a limited company formed of accumulated profits, which may be distributed to its members in due course.

reversion

The right of occupation which returns to the owner of freehold property on the expiry of a lease.

reversionary right

In copyright law, the return of a dead person's copyright to his relatives after a certain period of time, in spite of any agreement to the contrary.

reversioner

A person who enjoys an interest in land which will continue

after a person with a lesser interest such as a tenant has ceased to occupy it.

revival

The act of bringing back into validity a will which has been revoked other than by destruction.

revocation

The withdrawal of an offer in contract.

revocation by destruction

The effective revocation of a will by or on behalf of its maker (and in his presence), by intentionally burning, tearing or otherwise destroying it.

revocation by marriage

The principle that a will is revoked by the subsequent marriage of the person making it, unless it is expressed to be in contemplation of marriage.

revolving credit agreement

An agreement by which the borrower can continue to draw and repay money up to a certain limit, as opposed to the loan of a fixed sum.

rewards for stolen goods

It is a criminal offence to advertise for the return of stolen goods in terms suggesting that no questions will be asked if they are recovered.

right of abode

For immigration purposes, the right of a person to live in the United Kingdom.

right of angary

The right of any country in time of war to take over property on its territory, subject to compensation.

right of approach

In international law, the right of a warship to approach a vessel in order to verify its nationality.

right of audience
> The right to speak or conduct a case in court enjoyed by a litigant in person, by a barrister in the higher courts, and by a barrister or solicitor in the lower courts.

right of convoy
> The right claimed in time of war by some states to search neutral ships which are in convoy under the protection of their own navy. The United States is an advocate of the doctrine.

right of support
> The right of a landowner not to have the support of his building or land affected by activities on adjoining land.

right of visit
> In international law, the right of a belligerent ship in time of war to stop a neutral merchant ship, and check whether it is assisting the enemy in some way.

ring
> A combination of business interests to regulate the supplies of a class of goods so as to raise its price.

riot
> An unlawful assembly which is in the act of carrying out its objectives by force.

riparian owner
> The owner of land on one bank of a river or stream, whose rights extend half-way across the river bed.

riparian rights
> The rights enjoyed by the owner of land adjoining non-tidal waters.

Road Traffic Reports
> A series of decisions on road traffic cases of importance in injury claims and driving prosecutions.

robbery
> Theft carried out by force, or the fear of force.

Romalpa clause

A provision inserted in commercial contracts attempting to keep ownership in goods until particular conditions have been fulfilled.

Roman law

The system of law originated by Justinian, Emperor of Rome, from which many modern legal systems in continental Europe derive.

rosa solis *(Lat.)*

A spirit compounded with the juice of the sundew or rosa solis plant.

round charter

An agreement by which a ship is chartered for an entire round trip.

rout

An unlawful assembly which has made a start towards achieving its objective.

Royal Assent

The formality by which the sovereign consents to a Bill which has passed through both Houses of Parliament. It thus becomes an Act, and passes into the law of the land.

Royal Commission

A body appointed to conduct a thorough investigation of a particular problem or area of law, and to make recommendations for new legislation.

royal prerogative

A doctrine of common law by which servants of the Crown are appointed without being first obliged to obtain the authorisation of Parliament.

royal prerogative of mercy

The right of the Crown to grant a reprieve or pardon to a person sentenced for a criminal offence.

rubric

A passage in an ancient law book given emphasis by being penned in red.

rule against accumulations

A rule to prevent the accumulation of income from property under a direction in a will, beyond prescribed periods; in particular *(1)* 21 years from the death of the maker of the will; *(2)* the minority of anyone living at the maker's death; *(3)* the minority of certain other people.

rule against perpetuities

A doctrine establishing that the vesting of a particular property in a person may not be delayed beyond the period of his life, and 21 years after it.

Rule Committee

A body made up of certain judges and senior members of the legal profession, which draws up the rules governing the operation of the SUPREME COURT OF JUDICATURE (q.v.)

rule of law

The principle that all citizens of this country are subject to the same laws, and that no one can be punished for something not expressed to be illegal.

rules

A form of DELEGATED LEGISLATION (q.v.) made by Ministers, usually requiring submission to Parliament prior to coming into force.

Rules Committee of the Supreme Court

The body responsible for reviewing and issuing the rules of procedure for the Supreme Court.

rules of navigation

The internationally accepted principles which control the movement of ships navigating near enough to each other for a collision to be possible.

rummage

The searching of ship by customs officers to ensure that no prohibited or dutiable goods are on board.

S

Salford Hundred Court of Record
A court which exercised local jurisdiction in civil cases from medieval times until 1971.

salvage
The reward payable by the owners of a ship or its cargo to any persons saving it from wreck, capture or loss, who are under no obligation to take such action.

salvage agreement
A contract by which the person in charge of a ship in distress accepts the services of people offering to rescue it.

salvage lien
The right which a salvaging vessel enjoys over anything which it has rescued at sea.

sans frais *(Fr.)*
An indication that a person signing a commercial document such as a BILL OF EXCHANGE (q.v.) does not wish to accept liability for expenses.

sans recours *(Fr.)*
An indication that the person signing accepts no responsibility.

satisfaction
The doctrine that where there is no obligation to do a particular act, the carrying out of a different but equivalent act is deemed to be in substitution for the original obligation.

scale discharge

The terms under which bulk cargo from a ship is discharged as laid down in the chartering agreement.

scandalizing the court

The criminal act of doing something or publishing something designed to bring a court or judge into contempt, or to lower his or its authority.

scavage

Dues formerly paid by foreign merchants to the Corporation of London on goods brought into the City for sale. It was ablished in 1833.

Schedule D income tax

Particularly important as the classification under which self-employment is assessed to income tax.

Scheduled Territories

The countries which comprise the Sterling Area for the purposes of **EXCHANGE CONTROL** (q.v.), now abolished. Payment of sterling outside these territories could only be made with Treasury consent.

Schedule E income tax

The classification under which income from employment is assessed to tax.

scienti non fit inuria *(Lat.)*

A claim which may be raised in a civil court case, alleging that the defendant incurs no liability, because the person claiming was aware of the situation and took no steps at the time.

scheme of arrangement

(1) A settlement between a debtor and his creditors entered into after the start of bankruptcy proceedings.

(2) A procedure for altering the rights of a class of shareholders in a company.

sciens *(Lat.)*

Aware.

scintilla *(Lat.)*
A spark; an instant in time.

Scottish Bill
A Bill before Parliament certified as dealing entirely with Scottish matters, which may be dealt with by the SCOTTISH GRAND COMMITTEE (q.v.)

Scottish Grand Committee
A STANDING COMMITTEE (q.v.) of the House of Commons which, unless objection is raised, meets to consider matters exclusively Scottish.

sea coals
Coal arriving coastwise to the Port of London from Newcastle and neighbouring ports.

seaman's articles
A seaman's formal documentation containing his contract of service.

seaman's lien
The rights which a merchant seaman enjoys over ship and cargo as security for his unpaid wages.

seaman's will
A will made by a seaman at sea in respect of which strict requirements as to age and written formality are relaxed.

search warrant
An authorisation granted by a justice of the peace on sworn information permitting the entry and search of named premises.

Second Clerk Assistant
A permanent official of the House of Commons.

second mortgage
A further tendering of his property as security for a loan by a landowner who has already taken out a mortgage on that property.

secondary evidence
>Non-original or substituted material put forward as a means of proof.

Secretary-General of the United Nations
>The chief executive officer of the UNITED NATIONS (q.v.), in effect the head of the international civil service.

secret commission
>A bribe or inducement wrongfully taken by an agent to the detriment of the PRINCIPAL (q.v.) for whom he is operating.

secta
>In the Middle Ages, a group of supporters of the person bringing a case, who would give evidence as witnesses on his behalf.

secured creditor
>A creditor in a more favourable position at the winding-up of a company, whose debt is secured against specific assets which must be realised in his favour.

secured debenture
>DEBENTURE CAPITAL (q.v.) issued in respect of a loan where some or all of a company's assets have been mortgaged as security.

Security Council
>One of the principal organs of the UNITED NATIONS (q.v.). With a limited number of members, it has prime responsibility for maintaining international peace and security.

security for costs
>An order that one side to a civil action should be made to give some guarantee that costs incurred can be paid.

secus *(Lat.)*
>On the contrary.

se defendendo *(Lat.)*
>Applied to an act done in self-defence.

sedition

Malicious words, deeds or writing which do not in themselves amount to TREASON (q.v.), but which actually cause or are intended to cause discontent, civil disturbance, or hatred of the Queen or Government.

seditious conspiracy

A criminal offence committed by anyone who agrees with another person to carry out any act in furtherance of a SEDITIOUS INTENTION (q.v.) which both have.

seditious intention

For the purposes of criminal law, the intention to bring the institutions of the state into hatred or contempt, or to stir up disaffection or disorder against them.

seditious libel

The criminal offence of publishing anything capable of being a LIBEL (q.v.) with the intention that it should amount to SEDITION (q.v.)

sed quare *(Lat.)*

Generally used as a suggestion that the correctness of a particular statement should be questioned.

seduction

The act of persuading a female to have sexual relations, which formerly gave a right of action to a person who had responsibility for her.

seignorial court

An ancient court presided over by the lord of the manor, and dealing with disputes concerning those lands.

seisin

An old-fashioned word used to denote some form of ownership of land.

seizure

The act of taking possession of a thing by lawful authority of the State.

Select Committee

A parliamentary committee appointed to consider a specific Bill, sometimes by hearing evidence from witnesses.

Select Committee on House of Commons Services

A body which advises the SPEAKER OF THE HOUSE OF COMMONS (q.v.) on the support facilities used by the House of Commons.

Select Committee on Procedure

The committee of the House of Commons which regulates its public business.

Select Committee on Statutory Instruments

A committee of the House of Commons which deals with the DELEGATED LEGISLATION (q.v.) passing through the House.

selected action

Where there are several cases against the same defendant in the same court which arise out of the same circumstances, the defendant may apply for all the others to be postponed while the selected case is tried.

self-billing

The practice in VALUE ADDED TAX (q.v.) administration of customers receiving approval to make out tax invoices on behalf of their suppliers.

self-executing

Used to describe laws made outside the United Kingdom which take effect in this country without having to pass through Parliament.

self-governing colony

A colonial territory having a responsible government of its own.

self-supply

The use by a person registered for value added tax for his own purposes of goods or services which he would normally supply in the course of his trade, and which are therefore liable to tax.

semble *(Fr.)*

Apparently.

Senate of the Bar

The body governing the barristers' profession.

sentence

The penalty imposed by a court following a plea of guilty or a finding of guilt in a criminal case.

separation agreement

A formal pact between husband and wife that they should not live together.

separation of powers

The theory that there are three branches of government—legislative, executive and judicial—which must never duplicate each other.

sequestration

A writ against a person disobeying a court order which allows a number of people to take possession of his property until he complies with the order.

seriatim *(Lat.)*

Taking each point in a series one at a time.

Serjeant-at-Arms

In the House of Commons, an official who attends upon the Speaker; in the House of Lords, an official who attends upon the Lord Chancellor.

Serjeant-at-Law

A rank of senior barrister which existed until 1877, from among whom the judges were chosen. They were the forerunners of the modern QUEEN'S COUNSEL (q.v.).

service

The means by which official documents are brought to the attention of a particular individual, for example by personal delivery.

serviceman's will
> A will made by a soldier or airman on active military service in respect of which strict requirements as to age and written formality are relaxed.

service occupancy
> A requirement that an employee should live on certain premises so that he can carry out his tasks more effectively.

servient tenement
> Land subject to a PROFIT À PRENDRE or an EASEMENT (q.v.) such as a right of way.

session
> One of the periods into which the Parliamentary year is divided.

Sessional Committee
> A Parliamentary select committee which enjoys a certain degree of permanence in its make-up.

set-off
> A cross-claim made by the defendant that a particular sum owed by him to the claimant should be taken into account.

settled land
> Land subject to any kind of settlement which restricts the succession to it.

settlement
> The period on the Stock Exchange within which settlement for transactions must be made, or carried over into the next account.

settlor
> One who creates a trust by deed or will.

severability
> Applied to parts of an agreement which may be cut out by the court which is considering it, so that the remainder can be enforced.

several fishery

A private fishing right dating from time immemorial, or granted by statute.

severalty

Something held by a single person, rather than a shared ownership.

severing the indictment

An order to split criminal charges brought on one INDICTMENT (q.v.) into separate trials, on the basis that they are not sufficiently connected.

share

The interest of a shareholder or member of a limited company, as measured by an amount of money.

share capital

The nominal value of shares actually issued in a limited company.

share certificate

A certificate issued under the common seal of a limited company establishing the ownership of the registered holder to the shares referred to.

share-hawking

The practice, now forbidden by criminal law, of fraudulently attempting by direct approach to persuade people to buy shares in worthless companies.

share-pushing

The action, forbidden by criminal law, of fraudulently attempting to induce people to invest in worthless companies by advertisement or circular.

shares at a discount

The issue of company shares on the condition that the entire liability of the shareholder is less than the full nominal value of the shares. This practice is illegal without the authority of the Court.

shares at a premium

Company shares issued at a price above the nominal value of those shares, which does not need the consent of the Court.

share premium account

The account which a company is obliged to maintain if it issues SHARES AT A PREMIUM (q.v.), in which amounts equivalent to premiums must be lodged.

share warrant

A document which may be issued by a public company stating the entitlement of the bearer to the shares referred to, and to any dividends. As a negotiable instrument, it is transferable like a cheque.

shebeen

Premises in which unlicensed alcoholic drinks are sold.

sheriff

An ancient office in each shire or county which formerly involved great powers in such matters as law enforcement and tax collection. Now much reduced in function.

Sheriff Court

A Scottish court having limited jurisdiction in both civil and criminal matters.

Sheriff's Court

A court conducted by the High Sheriff or Under-Sheriff to assess damages where a person has allowed judgement in default to be signed, or to assess the worth of the land of a person unsuccessful in a court action.

Sheriff's Tourn

A local court of the Middle Ages enquiring into petty crimes.

shipmaster's lien

The rights which the captain of a ship enjoys to retain the cargo as security for the payment of the seamen's wages.

shipment

The actual placing of goods on a vessel or other means of transport.

shipowner's lien
> A LIEN (q.v.) which a shipowner has over goods which he has carried on a sea passage, against the payment due to him.

shipped bill of lading
> A BILL OF LADING (q.v.), which is made out only once the goods to be carried have been stowed on board the vessel.

shipper
> The person who consigns or delivers goods to a vessel or aircraft for transportation to a particular destination, for a particular charge.

shipping agent
> A person who represents a shipping company at a particular location or territory.

shipping bill
> A document in prescribed form which the exporter of dutiable goods or restricted goods must produce for examination prior to shipment.

shipping note
> Documentation accompanying goods delivered to the place of shipment for export.

shipping value
> In insurance matters, the cost of the goods paid by the person insuring them, plus shipping and insurance costs.

ship's articles
> The document which contains the agreement between the captain of a ship and its crew.

ship's marks
> Details of names, port of registry, tonnage and draught which must be marked on a ship prior to registration.

ship's master
> The person appointed by the owner of a registered British ship to be in charge of it; the captain.

ship's report

A document in prescribed form which the master of a ship must lodge in duplicate at the port of arrival, giving details of crew and cargo.

ship's stores

Dutiable goods permitted to be shipped duty free for use by crews of vessels leaving a United Kindom port for an overseas destination.

shire court

An ancient form of court in which the sheriff, as representative of the king, tried more important civil and criminal cases in each county.

Short Cause List

A list of cases for hearing in the Queen's Bench Division triable by jury and estimated not to exceed 2 hours.

short committal

A formal hearing before magistrates at which written statements and documentary evidence of a serious crime is handed in prior to trial by jury.

short term policy

A policy of life assurance payable only if death takes place within a specified period.

short title

The title by which an Act of Parliament is usually known.

show how

Information of a technical nature which can be best conveyed by instruction given to an individual while a job is in progress.

show of hands

The manner of voting normally used on any question put before the meeting of a company. Persons dissatisfied may demand a POLL (q.v.)

sic *(Lat.)*

Used to indicate how something was originally written,

generally indicating some fault in the later version. (Literally 'thus').

sickness benefit
> A state benefit payable to people who are normally employed or self-employed, but who are unable to work due to sickness.

sight draft
> A bill of exchange endorsed 'cash against documents' or C.A.D. (q.v.)

sighting
> The act of presenting a BILL OF LADING (q.v.) to a ship's master so that release of the goods may be obtained.

Sign-Manual
> The procedure by which on the signature of the Sign-Manual by a Minister, the royal will is deemed to be exercised.

Silk
> A popular term for a senior barrister who has been admitted to the rank of Queen's Counsel (Q.C.)

similiter *(Lat.)*
> Similarly.

simple contract
> A contract where no special form is needed, only the presence of CONSIDERATION (q.v.)

simplex commendatio non obligat *(Lat.)*
> A mere recommendation is not binding.

simpliciter *(Lat.)*
> Without any qualification; quite simply.

sine die *(Lat.)*
> Indefinitely; without a day being appointed.

single bond
> A personal security for the payment of money or the carrying out of some other act which has no condition attached to it.

single premium policy

A policy of life assurance by which only one premium is paid, at the time that it is taken out.

sinking fund

A sum of money set aside for the eventual repayment of a debt.

sister ship clause

A clause in a policy of marine insurance making the UNDER-WRITERS (q.v.) liable to the owner of a ship colliding with another ship owned by the same person.

sittings

The venue of a particular court, or the date and time at which it sits.

skimming

The removal of damaged goods from a particular container, so that only undamaged goods are left.

slander

Defamation in a non-permanent form, such as words or gestures.

slander of goods

A form of INJURIOUS FALSEHOOD (q.v.) giving rise to a civil action for wilfully disparaging the merits of another trader's goods.

slander of title

A form of INJURIOUS FALSEHOOD (q.v.), giving rise to a civil action for wilfully casting doubt on another person's entitlement to property.

sleeping partner

A member of a partnership who assumes no responsibility for the running of the business.

slip ('the slip')

A document prepared by an insurance broker noting the

terms of a proposed policy of marine insurance, and initialled by underwriters to the extent of any risk they are prepared to accept.

slip rule

The procedure by which an accidental error or ommission in a court's judgement can be corrected.

small beer

A weak table beer, originally sold at a duty-inclusive price of six shillings (30p) per barrel or less.

small claims court

Either the Registrar's court within a county court, which hears claims under a certain limit, or special courts which may arbitrate in such cases with the agreement of the parties.

smuggling

The criminal offence of importing or exporting goods without paying the duty, or in contravention of a prohibition.

snake

An agreement between certain European countries to limit the fluctuations of their currencies in relation to each other.

sodomy

Sexual intercourse by a male person involving anal penetration of either a man or a woman.

sold note

A contract note sent by a seller to a buyer setting out terms and conditions of an oral contract.

sole licence

Usually relating to patents, where the owner of the patent licenses the use to a single person, but himself retains the right to use it.

sole proprietor

A person working on his own account as a business, and not as a company or in partnership.

solicitor
> A member of one of the two branches of the legal profession. He has direct contact with the public, and generally undertakes a wider range of work than a barrister.

Solicitor-General
> One of the two Law Officers of the Crown in England and Wales, and a political appointment. He deputises for the Attorney-General in his capacity as adviser to certain Government departments and as prosecutor for the Crown.

Solicitor-General for Scotland
> The junior of the two Law Officers of the Crown in Scotland; it is a political appointment.

solus agreement
> A commercial contract by which one side agrees to take all its supplies from the other side.

software protection
> The doctrine that computer software, such as programs, can be subject to legal protection from copying via the copyright or patent systems.

sound recording
> The music, song or other sounds fixed onto a gramophone record or tape; in the United Kingdom it may be subject to a form of protection under copyright legislation.

South-Eastern Circuit
> One of the six circuits of the Bar of England and Wales.

South Sea Company
> Incorporated in 1711 by charter and enjoying the sole British trade round southern America from the Orinoco on the East, to the most northerly Spanish possessions on the West. Its rights were abolished in 1816.

sovereignty of Parliament
> The doctrine of the supremacy of Parliament, according to which Parliament can pass any law it pleases.

Speaker of the House of Commons
>   The chairman of proceedings in the House of Commons.

Speaker of the House of Lords
>   The effective chairman of the House of Lords, in principle the Lord Chancellor. In practice a number of other people often perform the function.

Speaker's Counsel
>   A permanent official of the House of Commons who services various committees and assists the CHAIRMAN OF WAYS AND MEANS (q.v.)

Speaker's Secretary
>   A permanent official of the House of Commons who looks after the Speaker's official arrangements.

special agent
>   A representative taken on by his principal for a particular purpose only, or for a single commission.

special commissioner of divorce
>   A senior barrister or holder of judicial office sitting with the powers of a High Court judge to try matrimonial cases.

special crossing
>   Its effect is that a cheque can be paid only to the bank nominated, or to another bank acting as its agent.

special damages
>   The sum of money actually needed to compensate an injured person for a particular loss.

special drawing rights
>   An arrangement between member states of the INTERNATIONAL MONETARY FUND (q.v.) to settle debts between themselves by drafts on a special fund.

special examiner
>   Someone appointed by a court to take the evidence of a witness (usually a witness unable to attend court in person).

special indorsement

An indorsement on a negotiable instrument such as a BILL OF EXCHANGE (q.v.) indicating to whom payment is to be made.

special manager

In bankruptcy proceedings, an official who may be appointed by the OFFICIAL RECEIVER (q.v.) to continue the business of the debtor.

special order

An instrument before the House of Lords which does not become law until it has received an affirmative resolution of both Houses of Parliament.

Special Orders Committee

A SELECT COMMITTEE of the House of Lords which considers every special order before that House.

special resolution

A decision passed by not less than three-quarters of the members present and voting at a company's GENERAL MEETING (q.v.), where not less than 21 days notice of intention to propose the matter as a special resolution has been given.

special verdict

A finding in a criminal case of 'not guilty but insane'.

specialty contract

A contract made by deed, requiring signature and sealing.

specialist select committee

A select committee of the House of Commons which sits to cover policy and administration in a particular field of specialisation.

specie *(Lat.)*

Money in coin, as opposed to paper money.

specific bequest

The gift of something in a will which can be definitely identified.

specific goods

> Goods which have been identified and agreed upon at the time that a contract is made.

specific performance

> An order that a person who is in breach of an obligation should be forced to carry it out.

spent conviction

> A previous conviction at some time in the past, which should not be taken into account in relation to the person concerned, particularly when he is being sentenced for a new offence.

spent lees

> The residue of the distillation of low wines in a pot-still distillery.

spent wash

> The remains of the distillation of wash in a distillery.

spes successionis *(Lat.)*

> A hope of inheriting something when another person dies.

spillage

> Applied to both solid and liquid goods which have accidentally come out of their containers.

spirits

> Any fermented liquor containing more than 40% of proof spirit.

spirits of wine

> Rectified spirits of the strength of not less than 43 degrees above proof.

spoilt beer

> Beer which has become unfit for use before retail sale, and which on return to the brewery is eligible for remission of duty.

spot price

> A price for immediate delivery and payment, as opposed to delivery and payment at some future time.

spot market

A market dealing in existing stocks for immediate delivery.

spying strangers

The procedure by which any Member of Parliament can have all members of the public and journalists removed from the chamber of the House of Commons.

squatter

A person who has entered into wrongful occupation of another person's land or premises.

stag

A speculator buying a new issue of shares, hoping that its price will rise because of over-subscription, so that he can sell at a profit.

standard of care

The degree of care which it is necessary for the defence to have shown in order to meet successfully an action for negligence.

standard rate

The normal rate at which VALUE ADDED TAX (q.v.) is charged on goods and services which are not exempt or ZERO-RATED (q.v.)

stand by for the Crown

The form of words by which the prosecution makes known an objection to a juror.

Standing Committee

A parliamentary committee which gives clause by clause examination to every Bill referred to it.

standing order

(1) An order made by either the House of Lords or the House of Commons to govern its own proceedings.

(2) A written authority from a customer to a bank, instructing it to pay a certain sum to a nominated person on a certain date.

Standing Orders Committee

A committee of either the House of Commons or the House of Lords concerned chiefly with matters related to private Bills.

Stannaries
>   Tin mining areas of Devon and Cornwall, the miners in which enjoy special privileges.

statement of capital
>   A document to be filed at the time of incorporating a company, stating its authorised capital for assessment of any duty.

statement of claim
>   A written statement setting out the facts on which a claimant in a civil action is going to rely.

state of the art
>   All material available to the public up to the filing of an application for a patent.

statement in lieu of prospectus
>   A statement to be filed by a company which has not issued a prospectus, to the effect that all directors have accounted for any liability on their shares.

Stationers' Hall Registry
>   A register of copyright books maintained by the Stationers' Company in London. No longer compulsory, registration there is still useful as evidence of rights.

status quo *(Lat.)*
>   The position unchanged.

status quo ante *(Lat.)*
>   The situation or position which existed previously.

stare decisis *(Lat.)*
>   The doctrine of judicial precedent, whereby the judgement of a court is binding on lower courts until overruled by a higher court or by Parliament.

statement of affairs
>   Documentary information to be sworn on oath to be presented to the OFFICIAL RECEIVER (q.v.) prior to the first meeting of creditors.

statute

A written law which has passed through first, second and third readings in both Houses of Parliament, and has received the Royal Assent.

statute-barred

The principle that legal rights which one person has against another shall be extinguished after a certain period of time.

statute law revision

The process of periodically weeding out obsolete Acts of Parliament.

statutory corporation

An undertaking such as the British Gas Corporation formed under special Act of Parliament.

statutory declaration

In company law, a statement filed on behalf of a company with the Registrar of Companies to the effect that certain preliminary conditions have been complied with.

Statutory Instrument

An order or regulation made under authority of an Act of Parliament which has the force of law.

statutory joint industrial council

A body which may be set up in particular trades or industries to regulate conditions of employment. It has equal representation of employers and employees.

statutory meeting

A general meeting of the members of a public limited company, which must take place within 3 months of commencing business.

statutory negligence

A breach of a duty imposed by Act of Parliament, as a result of which damage has been caused.

statutory report

A document which must be given to the members of a

company prior to the STATUTORY MEETING (q.v.) following commencement of business. It gives particulars of the administrative and commercial position of the company.

statutory tenant

A tenant who enjoys the protection of legislation against eviction and unilateral increases in rent.

statutory trust

The division of property left in a will equally between beneficiaries in a particular class.

stay

A putting into suspension of an order made by a court.

stay of proceedings

The bringing to a halt, either temporary or permanent, of a case being heard by a court.

Sterling Area

The SCHEDULED TERRITORIES (q.v.) for the purposes of EXCHANGE CONTROL (q.v.). Payments could only be made outside them with the consent of the Treasury.

stet *(Lat.)*

Used to indicate that a correction should be ignored, and the original used. (Literally 'let it stand'.)

still

Any equipment for distilling or making spirits.

store cattle

Cattle needing to be fed for at least 28 days before they are slaughtered.

stipendiary magistrate

A solicitor or barrister of at least seven years standing appointed as a paid magistrate to adjudicate in less serious criminal cases, instead of unpaid justices of the peace.

stockbroker

A member of the Stock Exchange acting on behalf of members of the public as agent for the sale and purchase of stock.

Stock Exchange ('the House')

A market for the purchase and sale of stocks and shares.

stop for freight

An application to the person having control of goods to hold them up until a carrier has been paid money owed for transporting them.

stop notice

(1) An order to a banker to stop payment on a cheque drawn by the account holder giving notice.

(2) In share transactions, a notice by someone having an equitable interest in shares to stop the transfer of shares registered in the name of another person.

stoppage in transitu

The right of an unpaid seller of goods who has parted with possession of them to stop them and repossess them before they have reached the purchaser.

straight bill of lading

A BILL OF LADING (q.v.) which cannot be negotiated, but under which goods must be delivered to a particular person named.

strandage

A toll formerly charged for depositing goods on a beach.

stranding

The running of a ship onto a seashore, which may be either accidental or deliberate.

street price

The price at which stocks and shares have been bought and sold in transactions outside the Stock Exchange, generally after close of business.

stress of weather

Bad weather conditions which may affect the carrying out of the terms of a contract.

strict liability

> In TORT (q.v.), absolute liability for the consequences of a state of affairs, irrespective of any fault or lack of care.

strict liability offence

> A criminal offence which can be committed without the guilty person having formed any criminal intent. Also known as an absolute offence.

strike clause

> A provision made in contracts by which it is sought to limit the effect of loss, damage or delay caused by industrial action.

striking off the rolls

> The act of depriving a solicitor of the right to practise, either as a disciplinary measure, or because the applicant seeks to become a barrister.

striking out

> The action of dismissing court proceedings, either in whole or in part.

strong waters

> An expression applied to all imported spirits other than brandy.

strict settlement of land

> A means of keeping landed estates within a family, primarily by creating successive life interests in favour of eldest sons.

sub-charter

> A contract made by a person chartering a ship to sub-let all or part of it to other people.

subject to contract

> A phrase indicating that the parties do not intend to be bound until a formal contract between them has been legally completed.

subject to equities

> The taking of a benefit subject to rights which may be enjoyed by third parties.

sub judice *(Lat.)*

Under judicial consideration. It is a serious contempt of court to enter into public discussion in the media of a matter in any case before the courts, which is therefore said to be sub judice.

submission of no case to answer

A submission by the defence, usually at the close of the prosecution case, that the prosecution has not shown a strong enough case to allow the matter to continue to be tried.

sub modo *(Lat.)*

In a limited way.

sub. nom. (sub nomine) *(Lat.)*

In the name of.

subordinate legislation

Orders, regulations and rules having the force of an Act of Parliament, but made by some body outside Parliament to whom the power to make them has been deputed by Parliament.

subpoena ad testificandum *(Lat.)*

A summons to compel a witness to attend court to give evidence in person.

subpoena duces tecum *(Lat.)*

A summons to compel a person having control of a particular document to produce it for a court hearing.

subscribed capital

That section of the shareholding of a limited company which has been paid for in cash.

subrogation

The substitution of one person for another as a creditor, and where the debtor has died, the right to stand in his executor's place. In insurance, the principle that an insurer who has paid out on a loss is entitled to the benefit of every right which the insured person would have.

subsidiary

A company under the control of another company either

through its board or by holding more than fifty per cent. of its shares.

sub silentio *(Lat.)*
Silently.

substantial damages
An award to compensate for the actual financial loss sustained by the injured person.

substituted service
The bringing of a court document to the notice of an individual by special steps, where normal service has proved impossible.

substitutional legacy
A gift by will in substitution for another gift, where it is clearly not intended that the two should be in addition to each other.

sub titulo *(Lat.)*
Under the name of; entitled.

sub-underwriting
An agreement by which a main UNDERWRITER (q.v.) contracts with other people to assume a proportion of his own potential liability.

succession
The transfer of a person's property on his death either by will, if he has made one, or according to legal rules if he has not.

sue and labour clause
A clause in a policy of marine insurance providing for the reward of efforts made by the master and/or crew to save the ship, should this be necessary.

Suez Canal clause
A clause in a policy of insurance providing that grounding of a ship in the Suez Canal is not to be regarded as stranding for the purposes of exclusion of liability.

suggestio falsi *(Lat.)*

A suggestion which is untrue.

suicide

The taking of one's own life.

suicide pact

An agreement between two or more people to bring about the death of all of them, irrespective of whether each person is to be responsible for taking his own life.

sui generis *(Lat.)*

Used to indicate that something belongs to a particular category.

sui juris *(Lat.)*

The condition of being of full age and thus able to sue and be sued in one's own name.

summary judgement

A means of avoiding full trial in a civil action under which the plaintiff claims that there is no defence to the action.

summary jurisdiction

Trial without jury exercised by a magistrates' court.

summary offence

A less serious criminal offence which can be heard only summarily before a magistrates' or justices' court.

summary trial

A trial in a magistrates' court before a stipendiary magistrate or justices of the peace.

summing-up

The review of the evidence and law given by the judge to the jury at the end of a criminal trial.

sum insured

The total amount which an insurance company is liable to pay under a policy of insurance.

summons

An order issued by a justice of the peace to a person accused of a criminal offence to appear before him on a particular day to answer the allegation.

summons for directions

Procedure by which directions are given by the Court as to the manner in which the trial of the main issue is to be conducted.

Superior Courts of Record

A classification embracing the SUPREME COURT OF JUDICATURE (q.v.), the House of Lords and the JUDICIAL COMMITTEE OF THE PRIVY COUNCIL (q.v.)

supervening impossibility

A situation where a contract is to be regarded as at an end because of some fundamental change of circumstances.

supervision order

A court order placing a child in need of care and protection under the supervision of a local authority.

support

A right which every piece of land is entitled to expect from land which adjoins it.

supplementary benefit

A state benefit payable to people aged 16 and over who are not working full-time, and who do not have enough to live on.

supplementary pension

A means-tested state benefit for people over pension age who do not have enough money to live on.

supplementary petition

A formal statement in divorce proceedings which may be used to bring up matters taking place after the case started.

supply

A parliamentary expression relating to the provision of finance to the Crown to fund the organs of the state.

supply services

Annual charges on state expenditure for such items as the armed forces and revenue collection departments.

supra *(Lat.)*

Above, in the sense of 'see above', where it appears in a piece of text.

Supreme Court of Judicature

This is made up of the Court of Appeal, the High Court and the Crown Court. (Not to be confused with the Supreme Court in the USA, as the English reference is often shortened to 'Supreme Court'.)

suppressio veri *(Lat.)*

A suppression of the truth (usually by omission of relevant facts).

surety

A person who undertakes to be answerable for the debt or default of someone else; also, the sum offered as guarantee.

suretyship

An undertaking or guarantee to answer for the debt or default of another person.

surplus stores

The unused remainder of goods which were permitted to be shipped duty-free for consumption by crews of ships sailing to foreign destinations from ports in the United Kingdom. Duty is chargeable on their return to this country.

surrender value

The amount which insurers are prepared to pay at any time in discharge of a life insurance policy.

survivorship

The principle that on the death of one of a number of joint owners of property, that property vests in the surviving owners.

suspended sentence

A punishment imposed by a court in respect of a crime by

which the offender does not go to prison unless he commits another crime within a certain period of time.

suspense account
> An account into which sums of money are paid on an interim basis, if for some reason they cannot immediately be paid into the account of ultimate destination.

sweets
> Any liquor made from fruit and sugar which has undergone a process of fermentation.

synchronisation right
> In copyright, the right to incorporate music in the soundtrack of a film.

syndicate
> An association of business interests.

T

Table A

A model set of articles of association annexed to companies legislation which a public limited company may adopt in whole or in part.

table beer

Beer sold in the 19th century at a price not exceeding 1½d. per quart.

Table Office

A department under the authority of the CLERK OF THE HOUSE OF COMMONS (q.v.)

Table of the House

The table in front of the Speaker's chair, at which the Clerk of the House of Commons sits.

tacking

The process by which a mortgagee may gain priority in repayment over any further loans.

tafia

A rum distilled in the French West Indies from the refuse (bagasse) of sugar cane.

tailings (feints)

The impure portion of the distillate from a low-wines still or general patent still.

take-over
>The merging of two companies by means of one company buying a controlling interest in the other.

take-over bid
>An offer circularised to members of a company offering to purchase their shares so as to give the person or company making the offer a controlling interest.

Take-Over Panel
>A watchdog body representing a number of financial institutions to ensure that procedures relating to company take-overs are not abused.

takings at sea
>The stopping on the high seas of neutral merchant ships, so that they may be taken into port for examination of cargo.

talis qualis *(Lat.)*
>'Such as it is.'

Tariff (the Tariff)
>A statement of all duties of customs and excise prevailing in the United Kingdom, now extended to cover the European Community.

tariff quota
>A system used in the Common Market to allow in products from outside the Common Market free of duty up to a numerical limit.

tattooing of a minor
>It is a criminal offence to tattoo a person under the age of 18 years.

taxation of costs
>The formal assessment of the costs of legal proceedings, according to a prescribed scale.

taxed costs
>The amount held by a TAXING MASTER (q.v.) to be payable by the unsuccessful party to a civil action.

Taxing Master

An official of the SUPREME COURT OF JUDICATURE (q.v.) who supervises the assessment of costs payable by the parties to an action. Appointed from solicitors of at least ten years' standing.

tax period

A period, generally of three months, in respect of which people registered for VALUE ADDED TAX (q.v.) must make a return.

tax point

The time when a particular charge to a tax becomes due. In relation to value added tax, the time when a supply of goods or services is made.

teller

A Member of Parliament appointed to count the number of Members voting in a division of the House of Commons.

tenancy

A leasehold interest in land, usually for a fixed term of years, and less than absolute ownership.

tenancy at sufferance

A situation arising where a person continues in possession after his contractual tenancy has come to an end.

tenancy at will

The grant of possession by an owner to a tenant for so long as either pleases, and terminable by notice or some act inconsistent with the tenancy.

tenancy from year to year

Tenancy created by grant or implication requiring six months notice.

tenancy in common

Where property is owned in agreed shares by several persons, and on his death the share of each owner passes to his PERSONAL REPRESENTATIVE (q.v.)

tenant for life

Someone entitled to enjoy the benefit of property during his own or someone else's life.

tender
>A response made to an advertisement asking for quotations to supply goods or to carry out works.

ten-minute rule
>The procedure under which a brief discussion of the case for and against the introduction of a Bill into the House of Commons can be made, in the hope that it will be sponsored later.

tents
>Sweet red wine from Spain.

term
>An expression describing elements of contracts of varying importance, such as CONDITIONS and WARRANTIES (q.v.)

term of years absolute
>A leasehold interest.

territorial straits
>Straits of land between which no HIGH SEAS (q.v.) exist, but where the intervening sea is entirely within the territorial limits of one or more countries.

territorial waters
>The area of adjacent sea over which a country claims to exercise territorial jurisdiction. The limits vary widely throughout the world.

testate succession
>The transfer of a person's property on a death according to the terms of his will.

testator *(Lat.)*
>A man who has made a will (as opposed to a female, known as a testatrix).

testatrix *(Lat.)*
>A woman who has made a will (as opposed to a man, who is known as a testator).

testatum *(Lat.)*

The clause in a conveyance or lease expressing the CONSIDERA-TION (q.v.) relating to the transaction.

test case

Where a number of actions are mounted against many defendants in respect of the same circumstances, one case may be selected to test the issues involved.

testimonium clause

The form of words by which a will is witnessed.

Test Roll

The book in which a new Member of Parliament enters his name, after taking the OATH OF ALLEGIANCE (q.v.)

theft

The dishonest appropriation of property belonging to another with the intention of permanently depriving that other person of it.

third party

A person not originally party to a case who has been joined to it because the original defendant claims that he is involved.

third party liability

The liability of an insured person to compensate someone who has sustained loss by his actions, or by the actions of persons under him.

third party proceedings

The process by which the defendant to a civil action claims that some third person and not himself is actually responsible.

thoroughfare town

An expression once applied to towns on the London-Dover and London-Berwick posting routes, where members of the Vintners Company of the City of London could sell wine without a justices' or excise licence.

three-fourths R.D.C. (running-down clause)

A clause in a policy of marine insurance making underwriters liable for three-fourths of any damage that the owner of the insured vessel may be obliged to pay to the owner of another vessel because of a collision.

threshold price

An expression used for Common Market purposes to denote the lowest price at which certain articles can be imported into the E.E.C.

through bill of lading

A BILL OF LADING (q.v.) which provides for the carriage of goods from one place to another by a series of forms of transport.

tied house

A public house subject to an agreement to buy all its beer from a particular brewery.

time charter

An agreement in the form of a CHARTERPARTY (q.v.) under which the ship is hired for a certain period of time.

time policy

A policy, generally of marine insurance, protecting the subject matter for a fixed period of time.

Times Law Reports

A series of reports of case decisions, no longer published, but still of importance. They should not be confused with those still appearing daily in *The Times.*

T.I.R.

Derived from Transport International Routier, this sign on a road haulage vehicle indicates that it has satisfied international convention requirements for security.

tithes

A tax payable to the Church in each parish, originally 10% of the value of the produce of a piece of land, commuted to a fixed sum of money in 1925, and now abolished.

tithing

In medieval times, a group of 10 men, the others of whom

would be responsible for bringing to trial one of their number who committed any crime.

title

(1) A summary of the purpose or intention of a Bill, which comes before the main body of the text.

(2) The right of ownership.

tobacco port

A port approved by the Commissioners of Customs and Excise for the importation of tobacco.

tolt

A writ used in the Middle Ages to bring a claim to recover land in the shire court.

Tolzey Court of Bristol

An ancient court of local jurisdiction in civil cases which was abolished in 1971.

tonnage and poundage

Legislation introduced at the Restoration to grant Charles II customs duties for the defence of English merchant vessels at sea.

tonnage dues

Charges made by a port authority on a ship entering its limits, which are calculated according to its registered tonnage.

tontine policy

A policy of life assurance where no bonus is payable if death takes place before the end of a stated period.

tort

Literally 'a wrong'; in law a breach of a duty created by the law, which gives rise to civil action at the hands of an aggrieved person.

tortfeasor

One who has committed a civil wrong giving rise to an action in law.

tortious act

An act giving rise to a cause of action for a civil wrong.

toties quoties *(Lat.)*
> As often as may be necessary.

towage
> The charge levied for the use of a tug to help a ship move in and out of harbour.

tower's liability clause
> In policies of marine insurance, a provision covering liability for damage caused while a tug is towing another vessel.

towing and salving clause
> A provision in a contract for the charter of a ship to cover the giving and receiving of tows, and other emergency situations.

town and country planning
> Legislation controlling the use of land by subjecting development to the sanction of the relevant local planning authority.

town customs
> Duties levied on goods by a city or town in former times, to maintain public works such as bridges, quays and harbours.

trade descriptions legislation
> Laws making it an offence to apply to goods a false description in the course of trading.

trade mark
> A mark used on or in connection with goods in order to demonstrate that they belong to the owner of the trade mark.

trade mark agent
> A member of the profession engaged in the process of obtaining recognition of TRADE MARKS (q.v.) by registration.

Trade Mark Register
> An official record of trade marks which is maintained at the Patent Office.

trading certificate
> A certification from the Registrar of Companies that a company is entitled to commence business.

tramp ship
> A trading vessel at liberty to carry freight all over the world, and not on any particular line.

transfer sessions
> Special sessions held by licensing justices in each district for the transfer of licences to sell alcoholic beverages.

transire *(Lat.)*
> A declaration giving details of his cargo which the master of a ship carrying goods around the coast of Britain must lodge with Customs and Excise prior to departure.

transit goods
> Goods on a ship or aircraft not to be delivered on arrival at a particular location, but to be carried further.

transmission clause
> A clause in a company's articles giving the personal representatives of a deceased shareholder the right either to transfer shares to themselves without registration, or to have themselves registered.

transmission of shares
> The automatic transfer of shares by operation of law in such circumstances as the death, bankruptcy or unsoundness of mind of the shareholder.

transshipment
> The transfer of goods between one vehicle, ship or aircraft and another before the final destination has been reached.

travaux préparatoires *(Fr.)*
> Preparatory drafts and discussions relating to legislation which may be considered in interpreting E.E.C. law, but not British Acts of Parliament.

traveller's cheque
> A draft drawn on a bank by the holder while away from home for a fixed amount.

traveller's letter of credit
> A request by an issuing bank to its associates abroad to issue cash to the holder up to a specified amount.

traverse
> In formally pleading a case, a contradiction of facts stated by the plaintiff.

treason
> A breach of faith or betrayal of allegiance owed to the reigning sovereign.

treasure trove
> A term applied to concealed gold or silver of which the owner is unknown, and which is accordingly deemed to belong to the Crown.

Treasury
> The Department of State responsible for administration and control of state expenditure.

Treasury Bench
> The front bench of the Government side in the House of Commons.

Treasury Bill
> A type of Government security which in 1897 replaced the Exchequer Bill.

Treasury Solicitor
> The head of his own staff of lawyers, and the most senior post in the GOVERNMENT LEGAL SERVICE (q.v.)

treaty
> A formal agreement between two or more countries.

Treaty of Accession
> The instrument by which the United Kingdom joined the Common Market (E.E.C.) in 1972.

Treaty of Rome
> The original agreement by which the Common Market (E.E.C.) was first established in 1957.

treaty port
> An expression formerly applied to places in China which were open to foreign trade.

treaty re-insurance
> An arrangement between insurers and re-insurers, by which the latter can accept or decline a proportion of any risk over the insurer's limit.

trespass
> An ancient form of action for physical injury or damage to property. No action can today be brought without proof of damage.

trespass by relation
> The principle that a person entitled to property can backdate an action for trespass to the beginning of his entitlement.

trespass de bonis asportatis
> An old civil action in respect of the wrongful taking of the property of another.

trespasser ab initio
> A person who originally entered by authority of law, but later abused it, and became a trespasser back to the moment of entry.

trespass on the case
> An old form of civil action in respect of indirect injuries.

trespass to goods
> The unlawful interference by one person with the property of another person.

trial by battle
> A method of trial in medieval times, by which one party to a case could fight in single combat for the justice of his cause, or nominate someone else to do it for him as his champion.

Trinity House
> The chief lighthouse authority in the United Kingdom, also

the pilotage authority for the Thames, English Channel and certain other areas.

Trinity Master

A senior member of TRINITY HOUSE (q.v.), who acts as nautical adviser in maritime cases.

trover

An ancient civil action for wrongfully disposing of another person's property.

truck

Payment in kind, by delivery of goods, which is an illegal act on the part of an employer.

trust

An interest in property, by which one person is bound in conscience to hold or administer property for the benefit of another person. To be distinguished from the American meaning of a monopoly or restrictive combination.

trust and personal representative costs

The basis of assessment of costs in legal proceedings where one of the parties is either a TRUSTEE (q.v.) or a PERSONAL REPRESENTATIVE (q.v.).

trust corporation

Corporations such as clearing banks, and some large insurance companies authorised to act as trustees.

trustee

A person bound in conscience to hold or administer property for the benefit of another person.

trustee in bankruptcy

A person appointed to administer the property of a bankrupt, and to distribute it among the creditors.

trust for sale

Created where it is ultimately intended that land shall be sold, but that the trustees enjoy the same powers as a tenant for life.

trust of imperfect obligation

A trust which cannot be enforced by a particular beneficiary, for example a pet cat in whose favour the trust has been established.

trust territory

A territory administered under the supervision of a country appointed by the United Nations.

turbary

An ancient right to dig turves on certain land.

turn

The difference between a dealer's buying price and selling price; particularly used about jobbers of securities.

turnover

The total sales of a business for a particular period.

turnkey agreement

In industrial contracts, an agreement for the supply of the complete range of material or equipment necessary.

turpis causa *(Lat.)*

Something dishonourable or immoral.

twopenny ale

A malt ale or beer much appreciated in Scotland in earlier times, so much that at the Union of Scotland and England, it was exempted from increases in duty.

two-thirds rule

The former rule that a JUNIOR BARRISTER (q.v.) appearing with a QUEEN'S COUNSEL (q.v.) was entitled to a fee of 2/3rds of that received by the Queen's Counsel.

U

uberrima fides *(Lat.)*
>   The principle that the most complete good faith should be used in making disclosures, particularly in relation to insurance contracts.

ubi jus, ibi remedium *(Lat.)*
>   Where a legal right exists, there is also a remedy.

ubi remedium, ibi jus *(Lat.)*
>   Where a remedy exists, there is a legal action.

ullage
>   The amount of liquid lacking in a barrel which is only partly full.

ultra vires *(Lat.)*
>   Any use of powers in excess of those laid down in governing documentation or legislation.

ultra vires borrowing
>   Borrowing by the directors of a company in excess of the limit authorised by its MEMORANDUM OF ASSOCIATION (q.v.)

umpire
>   An official who must be appointed where a matter has been referred to two or more arbitrators; he must give a decision if the arbitrators fail to agree.

unauthorised clerk

An employee of a stockbroking firm, not authorised to deal in stocks and shares on its behalf.

uncalled capital

That part of the value of shares in a limited company in respect of which full payment has not yet been demanded.

UNCTAD

The United Nations Commission on Trade and Development, which concerns itself with trading problems of developing states, particularly in the third world.

undefended divorce

A simple divorce case which is heard in the county court, the allegations not being contested by the other spouse.

under-insurance

Insurance for an amount less than the agreed valuation or the insurable value of property.

underlease

A later or sub-lease created by the occupier or tenant holding under the original lease.

underproof

The strength of spirits in which the proportion of alcohol is less than in proof spirit.

Under-Sheriff

The official deputising for the HIGH SHERIFF (q.v.)

underwriter

(1) A person undertaking to make the payment (the insurer) in a contract of marine insurance.

(2) Generally, a person undertaking to make up a deficiency, for example, the remainder of an issue of shares not taken up.

undischarged bankrupt

A debtor who has been declared bankrupt, and who commits a criminal offence if he obtains credit for more than a certain amount without declaring that fact.

undisclosed principal
> A person on behalf of whom an AGENT (q.v.) acts, but whose existence is not known to the third person at the time of making the contract.

undue influence
> Use by one person of a power over another person to induce the second person to take a certain course of action.

unemployment benefit
> A state benefit payable to people who are available for work, but who cannot find employment.

unenforceable
> The condition of not being enforceable by legal action.

UNESCO
> The United Nations Educational, Scientific and Cultural Organisation, a U.N. specialised agency, with its headquarters in Paris, which is responsible for international development in the areas referred to in its title.

unfair dismissal
> The right of an employee not to be unfairly dismissed by his employer, the breach of which gives a right of complaint to an industrial tribunal.

unicameralism
> The principle of having only one chamber or house in a parliamentary system.

unidentifiable cargo
> Goods which arrive at their destination so badly damaged that they cannot be identified.

unincorporated association
> A group of individuals existing to further common interests, for example a photographic club or a Chamber of Commerce, and which does not enjoy CORPORATE PERSONALITY (q.v.)

unitary state
> A country in which all power is concentrated in a central system.

United Kingdom

Generally, Scotland, England, Wales and Northern Ireland. It does not include the Channel Islands or the Isle of Man unless a particular Act of Parliament specifically extends to them for its special purposes.

United Nations Charter

The formal agreement to which states subscribing to the United Nations Organisation (U.N.O.) adhere.

United Nations Organisation (U.N.O.)

The current world association of independent states, founded after the Second World War, with its main headquarters in New York.

unit linked assurance

A policy of life assurance where most of the contributions are used to buy units in a unit trust.

unit of account

A device to establish single common prices for accounting purposes within the Common Market (E.E.C.)

unit trust

A managed trust by which subscriptions invited from the public are placed in a wide range of investments.

unity of invention

The principle that a successful application for a patent should relate to a single invention.

universal agent

An AGENT (q.v.) whose authority is completely unrestricted.

Universal Copyright Convention (U.C.C.)

One of the two major international copyright conventions, the U.C.C. requires lower standards of protection than the BERNE UNION (q.v.)

universal malice

In relation to murder, the intention to kill any of a group of people without aiming at a particular person.

unlawful assembly

A gathering of three or more people to do an unlawful act or cause a reasonable person to fear a breach of the peace.

unlawful sexual intercourse

The crime of having sexual relations with a girl who is below the age of 16; her consent to the act is no defence.

unlimited company

A company the members of which have no limit on their liability to contribute in the event of winding-up.

unliquidated claim

An allegation that an unfixed or uncertain sum of money is due.

unliquidated damages

Damages which the court itself fixes.

unneutral service

The act of a neutral merchant ship in time of war, which aids one of the belligerent countries in some way, or breaks a blockade.

unparliamentary language

Offensive words used in Parliament, which amount to a breach of order.

unsecured creditor

A creditor who has not taken any security from the borrower before making a loan or supplying goods on credit.

unsecured debenture

DEBENTURE CAPITAL (q.v.) which is not charged on the assets of a company, but taken only on the basis of a promise to repay the loan taken.

unseaworthiness

For the purposes of marine insurance, the condition of a ship which is unfitted to withstand the normal perils of the sea.

unvalued policy

An insurance policy which does not set a value on the items

insured, but leaves it to be fixed within the limits of the agreement.

usage

A particular course of dealing which is the normal practice in a certain occupation or area of business life.

use

An ancient right in EQUITY (q.v.) to the actual ownership of property, the possession of which is vested in another person.

usque ad centrum et usque ad coelum *(Lat.)*

'Down to the centre and up to the sky'—a maxim used to describe the rights attaching to ownership of land.

utmost good faith (uberrima fides)

The principle that a complete disclosure must be made of all relevant matters, particularly in relation to insurance.

usquebaugh (uisge beatha)

The Scottish Gaelic for whisky, literally 'the water of life'. It was applied to spirits distilled in Ireland and the Scottish Highlands, as opposed to spirits distilled in the Scottish Lowlands, which were known as 'aqua vitae' (also meaning 'water of life').

usufruct

A right to benefit from the yields of something owned by another person, without impairing the thing itself.

usury

The lending of money at an exorbitant rate of interest.

ut res valeat quam pereat *(Lat.)*

The principle that a thing should preferably be given effect rather than made void.

utter

To distribute something false or illegal.

V

v. (versus) *(Lat.)*
Against.

vacant possession
In respect of land or housing, the state of being free from occupation, so that a new owner or tenant can move in.

value added tax (V.A.T.)
An indirect tax charged on the supply of goods or services in the United Kingdom.

valued policy
A policy, generally in respect of marine insurance, setting out the agreed value of the subject-matter insured.

variable import levy
A device of the Common Market for the purposes of its COMMON AGRICULTURAL POLICY (q.v.), to bring prices of imports up to the level sought to be maintained inside the E.E.C.

variation of trust
A scheme for the re-arrangement of the terms of a trust in the interests of the beneficiaries.

V.A.T. return
The form on which people registered for V.A.T. (value added tax) must make a statement of their liability for each period.

vatting
> The admixing of spirits in a vat to secure uniformity of character.

V.A.T. Tribunal
> A special court established to adjudicate on appeals by the public against decisions of Customs and Excise on value added tax liability and assessment.

veil of incorporation
> The principle that a company is a distinct legal entity from its members.

venire de novo *(Lat.)*
> The power of a higher court to which an appeal is made to order a proper trial to take place, where the previous proceedings in a lower court were in some way defective.

venire facias *(Lat.)*
> The means by which a jury was summoned in the Middle Ages.

verbatim *(Lat.)*
> Word for word; applied to a record of something made 'exactly as it was said'.

verdict
> The decision reached by a jury or by magistrates as to whether or not a person is guilty of a criminal offence.

verification of flag
> In international law, the right of a warship to pursue and investigate another ship which is suspected of sailing under false colours.

verjuice
> Juice taken from sour grapes or apples which is unfit for making into wine or cider.

vertical integration
> The combining of a number of businesses, each following a different stage in the production process within the same industry.

vested legacy

A gift by will of personal property to be paid at a determinable time in the future, or when the recipient has reached a certain age.

vesting assent

A document vesting settled land in a tenant for life.

vesting order

In bankruptcy, an order made vesting DISCLAIMABLE PROPERTY (q.v.), in a person having an interest in it.

vexatious litigant

A person who persistently and without reasonable cause starts legal proceedings may be declared a vexatious litigant; he may then start cases only with the permission of a court.

vicarious liability

The liability of one person for wrongful acts committed by some other person.

vicarious performance

The situation where the person making a promise can rely on it being carried out by someone else.

Vice-Chancellor

A judge formerly appointed by the Lord Chancellor to take responsibility for the administration of the Chancery Division of the High Court.

vice-versa *(Lat.)*

'And the other way about'.

victualling bill

The document which a ship's captain must give to Customs and Excise before sailing for a foreign destination. It lists all dutiable goods to be used on the voyage.

vide *(Lat.)*

An indication in a text that the reader should consult the reference alluded to.

vi et armis *(Lat.)*
> In medieval times, a description for an act in breach of the
> KING'S PEACE (q.v.)

vinculum juris *(Lat.)*
> A legal tie.

virgo intacta *(Lat.)*
> A female whose maidenhead has not been broken by sexual
> intercourse.

virtute officii *(Lat.)*
> By virtue of some office held.

visible trade
> The export and import of goods (as opposed to services).

vis major *(Lat.)*
> Irresistible force making a particular act or event impossible.

viz
> That is to say.

void
> The state of being without legal effect.

voidable
> Capable of being made legally ineffective at the option of a
> particular person.

voir dire *(Fr.)*
> A preliminary examination of a witness or a juror, usually
> carried out by a judge, to see if the person involved is capable of
> fulfilling the particular function.

volens *(Lat.)*
> Willing.

volenti non fit injuria *(Lat.)*
> The principle that a person cannot bring an action for a civil
> wrong if he has consented to undertake the risk of damage or
> injury.

voluntary bill of indictment
> A means of bringing a serious criminal charge to trial in a Crown Court without going through COMMITTAL (q.v.)

voluntary excess
> The amount of any loss which a person taking out an insurance policy agrees that he will pay himself in the event of any claim which he makes.

voluntary manslaughter
> An expression covering cases reduced from murder to manslaughter because of PROVOCATION (q.v.), DIMINISHED RESPONSIBILITY (q.v.) and SUICIDE PACTS (q.v.)

voluntary winding-up
> The dissolution of a company brought about at the request of the company itself.

vote of censure
> A motion brought about by the opposition in Parliament expressing no confidence in the Government.

Vote Office
> The office of the House of Commons from which Members of Parliament obtain all their documentation.

vote on account
> The procedure by which the House of Commons authorises the interim spending of the Departments of State, until provision for their full annual expenditure is passed into law.

Votes and Proceedings
> The provisional record of the daily business of the House of Commons.

voyage
> For the purposes of maritime law, the trip out and the trip home taken together.

voyage charter
> A contract for the hire of a ship for a single voyage.

voyage policy

    A policy of marine insurance by which the subject-matter is protected for the duration of a specified voyage.

W

wager of law

> Also known as compurgation, a medieval form of trial by which teams of 'oath-helpers' gave ritual support to the parties involved in a lawsuit.

wagering contract

> A promise to give something to another person, on the ascertainment of an uncertain event in which neither has an interest. Not legally enforceable.

wager policy

> A form of insurance policy unenforceable in England, but not in some foreign states. The interest of the person insuring in the goods which have been insured is either very slight, or non-existent.

wages council

> A body which may be established in particular trades and industries to regulate pay, holidays and other working conditions.

waiver

> The situation where people who were in the course of entering an agreement decide to abandon their rights under it.

Wales and Chester Circuit

> One of the six circuits of the Bar of England and Wales.

want of age

The state of being below a particular age limit prescribed by law.

want of prosecution

The process by which a civil claim or criminal prosecution may be dismissed because the person making it has not taken the matter further.

war contraband

In international law, goods which may not be shipped to BELLIGERENTS (q.v.), without liability to seizure if captured.

war disablement pension

A state benefit payable to people who were disabled during wartime.

ward of court

A person taken under the care and supervision of the High Court for his or her own protection.

warehouse to warehouse

A policy of marine insurance by which goods are covered from the warehouse of consignment through the entire transit journey to final delivery at the warehouse of destination.

warehousing in bond

The system under which goods liable to duty can be deposited without payment of duty in a warehouse approved by Customs and Excise, when security for the duty is provided.

warned list

A list of cases likely to be tried in a particular court in the near future.

warrant of committal

An order of a court consigning a person to prison, generally for failure to obey the court.

warrant of delivery

An order of a court as a result of which one person is obliged to give goods up to another person.

warrant of possession

An order of a court to enforce a judgement for the recovery of land.

warranty

An element in a contract of less importance than a CONDITION (q.v.) Failure to meet a warranty will not bring the contract to an end, but may give rise to a liability to damages.

warranty of legality

A term implied into certain forms of contract, that all the circumstances surrounding the contract are legal.

warranty of neutrality

In policies of marine insurance, an implication that the vessel and its cargo will be of neutral character throughout a voyage.

war risks

In policies of insurance, the dangers stemming from actual military operations.

war widow's pension

A state benefit payable to widows and other dependants of people who died as a result of service in the armed forces.

wash

Distiller's WORT (q.v.) in which fermentation has begun.

waste

Unlawful damage committed or allowed by an occupier of land to the detriment of others having an interest in the land.

wasting asset

Property, the actual value of which diminishes as time passes, for example a leasehold running for a fixed number of years.

Watch Committee

Formerly, the police authority in a county borough.

Ways and Means

An expression relating to proposals in the House of Commons to authorise taxation and pay money into the CONSOLIDATED FUND (q.v.)

wear and tear
> Decay and deterioration in the course of normal use.

weather permitting clause
> In contractual agreements, a provision preventing time being counted where adverse weather conditions have prevented performance.

weather working day
> In contracts where performance depends on fair weather, a day on which work was not interrupted by adverse weather conditions.

weekly bills of mortality
> Weekly returns of births and deaths published in the parishes of London every Thursday prior to the establishment of the Register of Births, Deaths and Marriages in 1846.

Weekly Law Reports
> A modern series of current law reports published by the INCORPORATED COUNCIL OF LAW REPORTING (q.v.), and cited as W.L.R.

Weekly Notes
> A series of reports of legal cases which existed until 1952, and which are sometimes cited as case references.

weights and measures legislation
> Laws containing a general provision against the giving of short weight, even though no fraud can be proved.

Welsh Grand Committee
> A standing committee of the House of Commons which deliberates on matters which are exclusively of Welsh interest.

wer
> The medieval valuation of a person according to his station in life.

Western Circuit
> One of the six circuits of the Bar of England and Wales.

wharfage

A charge made for depositing goods on a wharf.

where equities are equal, the law shall prevail

The principle in EQUITY (q.v.) that if there are two or more claimants to a property, the person having the legal estate should succeed.

Whip

A member of a party in either the House of Lords or the House of Commons, who controls party business and organises voting arrangements.

White Book

The publication which contains the Rules of the Supreme Court.

White Paper

A governmental publication giving details of some topic which is to be laid before Parliament.

white slaving

The procuring of women for the purposes of prostitution, generally in some locality overseas.

whole account policy

A form of bad-debt insurance, covering losses up to an agreed percentage of total sales.

whole life policy

A contract of LIFE ASSURANCE (q.v.) where it is agreed that the sum assured is only payable on the death of the person whose life has been assured.

wholesaler

One who purchases goods in large quantities from manufacturers, and sells on to retailers in smaller amounts.

wholly owned subsidiary

A company which has no members other than another company which owns it.

widowed mother's allowance
>A state benefit payable to a widow of any age who has at least one child under the age of 19.

widowers' duty
>An assessed tax which was levied according to social position on all childless widowers not receiving charitable support. It lasted from 1695 until 1706.

widow's allowance
>A state benefit payable to widows under the age of 60 whose husbands are not receiving a retirement pension.

widow's pension
>A state benefit payable to women widowed at 40 or over, or who have no dependant children, or who are 40 or over when the WIDOWED MOTHER'S ALLOWANCE (q.v.) ends.

wilful neglect to maintain
>A type of allegation which can be made the subject of matrimonial proceedings. If brought, it may be defended by the other spouse, and a trial of the matter will take place.

wilful refusal to consummate
>The decision of one spouse never to allow the other to have sexual relations, which is a ground for ANNULMENT OF MARRIAGE (q.v.)

winding-up
>The normal method of dissolution of a company, either because of insolvency, or because the purposes for which it existed came to an end.

winding-up order
>A formal order made by the court for the dissolution of a company.

winding-up petition
>The formal means by which a compulsory dissolution of a company by the court is put into motion.

window duty

The number of windows in a house was the criterion for assessing the Inhabited House Duty from 1696 until that duty was abolished in 1834. Thereafter a window duty continued until 1851.

wine lees

Dregs of wine.

Witan

The king's advising council prior to the Normal Conquest, who were involved in framing the laws.

wite

In the Middle Ages, a fine payable to the king in respect of any wrongdoing, in addition to any compensation payable to the person injured.

woman named

The woman with whom the husband in matrimonial proceedings has committed ADULTERY (q.v.)

Woolsack

The official seat of the member of the House of Lords who is at any time acting as its SPEAKER (q.v.)

working capital

The excess of current assets over current liabilities.

workmens' compensation supplement

A state benefit payable to employees who had an accident at work or contracted an industrial disease before 5 July 1948.

World Health Organisation (W.H.O.)

A specialised agency of the UNITED NATIONS (q.v.) responsible for research and development in medical matters.

worm

A copper pipe connecting the head of a still with the safe in a distillery.

wort

The liquid obtained by dissolving sugar or molasses in water, or by extracting the soluble portion of malt or corn during brewing.

wreck

Generally applied to anything without an obvious owner, on or in the sea, or cast up by it.

wreckage

Any material which has been thrown up on a shore after a shipwreck.

wreck commissioner

A member of a special court set up to investigate a shipwreck.

wreck report

The details which must be given by the captain of any ship arriving in the United Kingdom, of any wreck or derelict vessel met during the voyage.

writ de cursu

A medieval writ issued in circumstances similar to those in respect of which a writ had previously been issued.

writ of assistance

A document issued to an officer of Customs and Excise authorising him to enter and search any premises.

writ of atteint

A medieval procedure by which a jury accused of bringing in a false verdict could be themselves tried by a second jury.

writ of summons

A document the issue of which commences a civil case in the High Court.

Y

Yaoundé Convention

An international agreement between the states of the Common Market and certain of their former territories, by which the latter are allowed certain tariff reductions on importation of their products into the E.E.C.

Year Books

Medieval notes of decided cases written in Norman French, now primarily of historical interest.

year's purchase

The rent, profit or income during a year, used as a method of valuation.

yield

The return on an investment from dividend or interest expressed as a percentage of its market price or cost.

youth custody order

A sentence of detention now imposed on a young offender for a specified period, in place of the previous Borstal order.

Youth Opportunities Programme

A fixed monetary allowance was payable under this scheme to school-leavers wanting to gain work experience or vocational training. Now replaced by the Youth Training Scheme.

Z

zero-rating

    Applied to a class of goods which are technically liable to VALUE ADDED TAX (q.v.),but for which the effective rate of tax is nil.

zone time

    A standard of time to be applied at sea, dependant on the time zone in which a vessel is positioned.